Tackling Poverty and Disadvantage in Schools

Other titles by Bloomsbury Education

The Ultimate Guide to Adaptive Teaching by Sue Cowley
Creating Belonging in the Classroom by Zahara Chowdhury
Time to Shake Up the Primary Curriculum by Sarah Wordlaw
Representation Matters by Aisha Thomas
Celebrating Difference by Shaun Dellenty
The Inclusive Classroom by Daniel Sobel & Sara Alston

Tackling Poverty and Disadvantage in Schools

Editors:
Sean Harris and Katrina Morley

BLOOMSBURY EDUCATION
LONDON OXFORD NEW YORK NEW DELHI SYDNEY

BLOOMSBURY EDUCATION
Bloomsbury Publishing Plc
50 Bedford Square, London, WC1B 3DP, UK
Bloomsbury Publishing Ireland Limited
29 Earlsfort Terrace, Dublin 2, D02 AY28, Ireland

BLOOMSBURY, BLOOMSBURY EDUCATION and the Diana logo
are trademarks of Bloomsbury Publishing Plc

First published in Great Britain, 2025 by Bloomsbury Publishing Plc
This edition published in Great Britain, 2025 by Bloomsbury Publishing Plc

A catalogue record for this book is available from the British Library.

ISBN: PB: 978-1-8019-9475-0; ePDF: 978-1-8019-9476-7; ePub: 978-1-8019-9478-1

2 4 6 8 10 9 7 5 3 1 (paperback)

Typeset by Newgen KnowledgeWorks Pvt. Ltd., Chennai, India
Printed and bound in the UK by CPI Group (UK) Ltd., Croydon, CR0 4YY

To find out more about our authors and books visit www.bloomsbury.com
and sign up for our newsletters.

For product safety related questions contact productsafety@bloomsbury.com.

Acknowledgements

We extend our deepest gratitude to all those who have contributed to the creation of this book.

First and foremost, we wish to express our heartfelt appreciation to our family members. Your unwavering dedication and steadfast support have been our bedrock throughout this journey. You inspire us daily and enable us to pursue our passions with vigour and purpose.

To the numerous thinkers and change-makers whose work we have featured in this book: your research, case studies and best practice examples have provided invaluable insights and significantly enriched this resource.

To our publisher, Bloomsbury Publishing, and the entire team: thank you for your profound commitment to the themes explored in this book. Your support at every step has been instrumental in bringing this project to fruition. We are immensely grateful to our book mentors, Cathy Lear and Joanna Ramsay. Your unwavering dedication and steadfast guidance have been vital in shaping this book and supporting us throughout its development.

Our sincere thanks go to each co-author and organisation who contributed to this book. Your collaboration, generosity with time, expertise and collaborative spirit have been exemplary and have profoundly enriched this work. The education sector is richer for having you in it.

Special recognition is due to Tees Valley Education, particularly our colleagues and the Trustees. Your time, commitment and vision for this project – as more than just a book, but as a means to further contribute to addressing educational inequality at scale – have been pivotal.

We also wish to acknowledge the networks and organisations that have strengthened us professionally. In particular, the Chartered College of Teaching, SHINE and the Fair Education Alliance have provided invaluable support and inspiration, for which we are profoundly grateful. A particular thanks to Dame Alison Peacock for providing the foreword for this book and for her uncompromising commitment to championing educators and the sector.

Finally, to every child and family we have served who has faced barriers due to poverty and hardship: you are not a problem to be fixed; you are a joy and a privilege to walk with. Your resilience and spirit are a constant source of inspiration, motivation and collaboration.

Sean Harris and Katrina Morley

This book is dedicated to all adults, children and young people
who have encountered poverty or disadvantage in any form.
It is further dedicated to the leaders, educators and organisations
committed to enhancing the opportunities of all children
through education.
Every child deserves a quality education and the best start in life.
Especially those children facing poverty and disadvantage.

Contents

Part 3: **Tackling poverty in other ways**

Foreword

This is an important book. What shines through every chapter is a 'can do' approach to tackling the pernicious effects of poverty on children's lives. The sense of collegiality, collaboration and a refusal to accept the status quo are evident in every chapter. This is an illustration of positive steps that are being taken in communities across England to address the worst effects of disadvantage and marginalisation amongst our children. This is not an exploration of government policy; instead it is a testament to teachers, school leaders and third sector organisations who are doing their utmost to help. Often, in addition to practical steps, it is a mindset that refuses to accept inequity that makes the most difference. When I was studying for Learning without Limits, the key issue was one of shifting colleagues away from deterministic assumptions to notions of opportunity and equity. Refusal to accept so-called 'ability-based' approaches to teaching and learning chimes strongly with a similar refusal to accept that lack of material advantage should be allowed to impact children's access to education.

In the first five chapters, ways to adopt a 'whole-school' approach to tackling poverty and disadvantage are explored, taking practical examples from schools and MATs (multi-academy trusts) who are actively making a difference in their communities. Teachers at North East Academy Trust (NEAT) take the view that the better they know families in terms of strengths and barriers, the better placed they are to help via a relational, whole-family approach. NEAT has the mantra:

'Know our children well, know our families and community well, know each other well.'

At Northampton Primary Academy Trust (NPAT), they understand that contextual professional development of teachers is a significant lever for change in schools and that high-quality CPD (continuing professional development) has a greater effect on pupil attainment than other interventions (Fletcher-Wood and Zuccollo, 2020). In response, they invest in a Lead Teacher Educator in every school, thereby maximising the effectiveness of the most expensive asset any school has – teachers. At the Chartered College of Teaching, it is this philosophy that drives our charitable purpose: we know that the more we can support teachers in their endeavour to make a difference, the more impactful they can be.

In Chapter 3 we learn about a study by Children North East (2011), where 1,000 children used cameras to document their lives, giving researchers the opportunity to understand much about unintentionally stigmatising issues that form barriers to learning and participation in and around school. The importance of 'early help' and intervention via multi-agency support is discussed in Chapter 4, noting that poverty and disadvantage are multifaceted and potentially therefore amongst the hardest challenges schools have to face. A culture of high support and high challenge at Loughborough Primary School is offered as an inspirational case study of what can be achieved through a multi-agency approach.

Chapter 5 shows us how pupils can be pivotal in helping the wider community to understand their circumstances, and how schools such as Bede Academy are able to defy expectations through offering inspirational stories of pupils achieving and attaining highly. Evlina's painting is one of the highlights of the book – her beautiful artwork powerfully illustrates the capacity of asylum seekers and refugees to achieve when greeted with the warmth of a welcoming whole-school ethos, such as that at Bede Academy.

The next four chapters focus on the classroom and the difference that teachers make. We learn about the impact of poverty on the learning brain, which may affect memory and processing skills. However, authors are keen to stress that we must avoid assumptions that poverty necessarily impacts innate capacity to learn. Advice is offered about the benefits of low-stakes quizzing, self-explanation and the consolidation of key concepts whilst minimising cognitive load. The power of curriculum planning, building key knowledge and concepts is discussed in Chapter 7, and in Chapter 8 the importance of culture is explored, with the authors making the vitally important point that 'culture is infectious'. Poverty, reading and literacy are discussed in the final chapter in this section. We are reminded of the statistics published annually by the National Literacy Trust about book ownership; the stark facts about the opportunity gap are shown. Again, the positive action-oriented approach of this book is to explore what can be done to swim against the tide, using the teaching of reading as an inviolable right for every child.

The first chapter in the final section discusses the link between poverty and school exclusion, showing the magnitude of this problem and calling for proactive rather than reactive policies. The benefits of collaboration and partnerships are explored in Chapter 11 with a theory of change model applied to charitable giving, seeking the multiplier effect for greatest impact. The potential for an individual tutoring system to identify barriers to learning through building trust via ACE (A Champion for Every Child), as deployed by

The Kemnal Academies Trust (TKAT), offers another inspirational, strengths-based model. The resourcefulness and energy of such schools is such a source of hope. We learn about the huge impact of careers-related learning in a hyper-local context in Chapter 13. We are offered a powerful example of a curriculum planned in partnership locally to ensure that key concepts are connected to points of local relevance in the business world. Importantly, the final chapter offers examples of research and school–university partnerships that build new knowledge and capacity to engage with real-world issues.

There is so much within this book that will be of everyday use for individual teachers wishing to enact equitable classroom practice, but the most powerful examples of action come from the collective – groups of schools and partnerships from a wide range of organisations, all coming together to enable a community-wide appreciation of what it is possible to achieve when we truly value each other. The promise of this book is that through drawing together ways of working that are proven to remove barriers, we can collectively do so much more to make a difference.

Thank you for all that you do to support our children.

Dame Alison Peacock
Chief Executive
Chartered College of Teaching

Introduction

We believe that you have chosen to read this book because you share our commitment to championing children's welfare and endeavouring to tackle poverty and disadvantage in your school community.

Tackling Poverty and Disadvantage in Schools is not about simplistic solutions. We know how important it is to understand and tackle head on the complexities of poverty and disadvantage within our communities. Both of us have encountered adversities, not only in our professional capacities but also within our personal lives. While our experiences do not make us experts in the impact of poverty, they have given us personal insights into the challenges posed by poverty, disadvantage and resource constraint in the pursuit of learning.

In writing this book, we have drawn on our own extensive experience within educational settings and diverse sectors, alongside a team of expert contributing authors. We acknowledge that a nuanced understanding is needed to navigate these complex topics and that expertise is cultivated through collaboration and partnerships both within and beyond the education sector. This book is the product of such collaborations with leaders, educators and organisations who ardently advocate for children and the pivotal role of schools.

Tackling Poverty and Disadvantage in Schools is intended as a practical resource that can be used by school leaders and teachers, governors, SENDCos and pastoral leaders across the sector, supporting you to:

- look beyond harrowing statistics that show the scale of poverty and disadvantage in the communities that schools serve
- identify and tackle the barriers to learning that can exist as a result of poverty and disadvantage
- further respond to poverty in your school(s).

The chapters provide overviews of useful research, case studies, ideas to try and reflective tasks, all aimed at addressing the multi-faceted poverty-related barriers to learning that our pupils might encounter.

Tackling poverty and disadvantage in schools and securing good outcomes for the children, families and communities in our care demands an unwavering commitment. But this cannot happen in a silo. We believe the best partnerships are founded not merely on shared objectives but on a collective commitment to fostering equity.

We went into education driven by a profound desire to effect positive change, and we surmise that you share this aspiration. Consider this book an invitation to learn and reflect alongside fellow professionals deeply invested in the welfare of children and the transformative potential of schools at the heart of their communities. Let us unite in understanding the complexities of poverty and endeavour to create meaningful change.

Sean Harris and Katrina Morley

How to use this book

The book is divided into three core strands:

- **Part 1:** Understanding and tackling poverty across the whole school
- **Part 2:** Understanding and tackling poverty in the classroom
- **Part 3:** Tackling poverty in other ways

Each strand is broken down into chapters.

Part 1

- **Chapter 1: Unpacking poverty in schools** – how to understand poverty and think more broadly than the pupil premium.
- **Chapter 2: Professional development** – how to develop a shared language of poverty in CPD, train staff and raise awareness of community needs.
- **Chapter 3: Poverty Proofing© the School Day** – how to tackle poverty as a whole school community, drawing on research carried out by Poverty Proofing© the School Day, with a particular focus here on food, clothing and activities.
- **Chapter 4: Early help and intervention** – how to tackle poverty through early help and intervention, working directly with children/young people, families and communities.
- **Chapter 5: Displacement and poverty** – how to support the needs of marginalised groups, with a key focus on refugee/asylum-seeking children.

Part 2

- **Chapter 6: Poverty on the brain** – how to apply research on neurology and poverty in practical ways in the classroom.

- **Chapter 7: Crafting curriculum** – how to design curriculum and character education with poverty in mind.

- **Chapter 8: Social justice and school culture** – how to champion social justice through whole-school and subject-specific approaches to extra-curricular opportunities.

- **Chapter 9: Reading and literacy** – how to tackle local need and poverty challenges through individual pupil, classroom and whole-school approaches to reading culture.

Part 3

- **Chapter 10: Tackling the cycle of exclusion** – how to support vulnerable and disadvantaged pupils at risk through behaviour and exclusion – preventative measures in schools.

- **Chapter 11: Partnerships** – how to build partnerships and make funding applications to attract investment in projects to support pupils/families.

- **Chapter 12: Mentoring** – how to support disadvantaged pupils to tackle barriers to learning using mentoring, drawing on evidence from the ACE (A Champion for Every Child) mentoring programme.

- **Chapter 13: Engagement with business and industry** – how to form partnerships with business, industry and enterprise leaders to support career pathways.

- **Chapter 14: Research collaboration** – how to form partnerships with universities to help tackle the impact of poverty in schools.

Chapter organisation

We know that teachers and leaders working in schools are busy and the day job is demanding, so we have designed the book with this in mind. Each chapter follows the same structure to make it easier for you to read it and reflect with colleagues.

	Research summaries	A summary of notable research or thinking that has supported the co-author(s) in understanding more about the topic of the chapter. This is designed as an introduction to the research, not a detailed explanation.
	Case study	A case study that looks into the theme of the chapter and approaches to tackling poverty using a real-world example.
	Ideas to try	A selection of actionable and road-tested ideas colleagues have used in different settings to tackle and address aspects of poverty.
	Recap and Reflective tasks	As teachers, we couldn't miss the opportunity to include a short quiz based on the chapter content. Answers are given at the end of the book. (N.B. The recap statements may not always fit into the simple binary of true or false, but we believe that this is a useful exercise in prompting thinking around the statement and helping your recall of the chapter content, so please choose the option which feels most accurate, including for your school setting.) Reflective tasks to use in schools or other settings with your colleagues will help you plan and strategise with the help of the ideas covered in the chapter.
	Further reading and Links	Suggested further reading on the chapter's topic and links to digital resources.

Online resources

Online resources are available at bloomsbury.pub/Tackling-Poverty.

Co-authors have shared resources that will support school leaders and teachers in further exploring the contents of the chapters in schools.

You can access these for free by scanning this QR code or following the link above.

Reading strands

You may want to read the whole book in one go. Don't let us stop you!

In the brief guide below we signpost chapter content that we think will be most relevant to specific roles in school.

Role(s)	Recommended chapters
Teachers and other adults working in classroom settings	1: Unpacking poverty in schools 6: Poverty on the brain 7: Crafting curriculum 8: Social justice and school culture 9: Reading and literacy
Curriculum and subject/ phase leaders	1: Unpacking poverty in schools 6: Poverty on the brain 7: Crafting curriculum 8: Social justice and school culture 9: Reading and literacy

Role(s)	Recommended chapters
Teacher educators and CPD leaders	1: Unpacking poverty in schools 2: Professional development 6: Poverty on the brain 7: Crafting the curriculum 9: Reading and literacy 14: Research collaboration
SENDCos or pastoral leaders	1: Unpacking poverty in schools 3. Poverty Proofing© the School Day 4: Early help and intervention 5: Displacement and poverty 10: Tackling the cycle of exclusion 11: Partnerships 12: Mentoring
Senior and system leaders	1: Unpacking poverty in schools 3. Poverty Proofing© the School Day 4: Early help and intervention 5: Displacement and poverty 7: Crafting curriculum 8: Social justice and school culture 10: Tackling the cycle of exclusion 11: Partnerships 12: Mentoring 13. Engagement with business and industry 14: Research collaboration
Headteachers	1: Unpacking poverty in schools 3. Poverty Proofing© the School Day 4: Early help and intervention 5: Displacement and poverty 8: Social justice and school culture 10: Tackling the cycle of exclusion 11: Partnerships 13: Engagement with business and industry 14: Research collaboration

Role(s)	Recommended chapters
Governors, trustees and other stakeholders	1: Unpacking poverty in schools 3. Poverty Proofing© the School Day 5: Displacement and poverty 8: Social justice and school culture 10: Tackling the cycle of exclusion

PART 1

Understanding and tackling poverty across the whole school

1 Unpacking poverty in schools

Debi Bailey, Sean Harris, Katrina Morley

Chapter summary

Poverty is arguably the most complex issue facing teachers and leaders working in schools. In this chapter, we will briefly explore the concept of poverty and consider why poverty and disadvantage need to be understood in schools beyond the scope of the pupil premium (PP) and free school meals (FSM) policies. We will discuss ways to establish a working definition of poverty and disadvantage: a vital part of a school-wide strategy to tackle poverty.

What does the research suggest?

A plethora of research exists about poverty. In this section, we have provided some of the research that has helped to broaden our understanding of poverty in our own schools and the effects of poverty-related barriers to learning. Some of this research has been vital in supporting leaders and teachers to look beyond the pupil premium policy as the main approach to understanding and tackling poverty in schools.

Research 1

Gorard et al. (2019)

'The difficulties of judging what difference the Pupil Premium has made to school intakes and outcomes in England'

The authors are education researchers based at Durham University Evidence Centre for Education (DECE). The paper highlights the challenges in assessing the impact of the PP due to various factors such as economic changes, legal definitions and metrics used to measure pupil outcomes. The authors suggest that previous research has sometimes overlooked these factors, making earlier estimates of the attainment gap unreliable. The work of DECE is helpful for school leaders and teachers wanting to understand why relying on PP data to measure and understand poverty in schools is problematic.

Key points

- A challenge for policymakers and schools is that the FSM-eligible group will sometimes contain pupils who have not been eligible previously.

- Changes in the definition of those known to have poverty-related barriers to learning therefore impact apparent attainment gaps.

- This study introduces a new analysis using data from the National Pupil Database, which accounts for changes in the prevalence of FSM eligibility and other factors. The findings reveal that the PP may be effective in reducing some aspects of attainment gaps in schools.

- The research concludes that the PP should continue in schools, but with further research needed to understand its long-term impact on the poverty gap.

- Additionally, the research recommends recalibrating the funding in education to be fairer to areas experiencing longer-term, sustained disadvantage in communities.

Research 2

Rowland (2021)

'Addressing Educational Disadvantage in Schools and Colleges: The Essex Way'

Marc Rowland works with the Unity Schools Partnership and alongside the Education Endowment Foundation's (EEF) national Research School Network. This book highlights research and insights from the Unity Schools Partnership, in collaboration with the local authority and a range of schools in Essex. The research is a helpful and practical reference in understanding how to tackle educational disadvantage at scale.

Key points

These are some of the key recommendations from the book:

- A forensic understanding of children and families facing poverty is needed in schools.
- Teachers and leaders need to understand how poverty and disadvantage impact pupils' learning in their context.
- The impact of poverty and disadvantage on learning is a process, not an event. A long-term view is therefore needed if schools are to tackle it.
- Schools which facilitate early help and intervention are more likely to be successful in both understanding and addressing poverty and disadvantage.
- Schools are well-placed to define and understand disadvantage in their context.
- Strategies to tackle educational disadvantage need to move beyond labels.

Research 3

Mullen and Kealy (2013)

'Poverty in school communities'

Mullen and Kealy are researchers based in the USA. They conducted research into poverty in schools and examined research papers from different states across the USA. The review provides a useful insight into literature on poverty issues in education and different types of poverty. The research explores practical considerations to help enable teachers to be poverty researchers in schools and therefore better understand contextual need. Supporting teachers and leaders to further understand and research poverty in their setting is explored in Chapter 14.

Key points

These are some of the important trends from the research:

- Teachers of SEND (special educational needs and disabilities) had a greater interest in poverty in schools than school leaders and other educators.

Researchers thought there was a possible correlation with the fact that teachers of SEND had greater contact with pupils from poverty.

- Teachers wanted to pursue a practical mindset towards both understanding and addressing poverty in their settings, but poverty alleviation is more than just raising pupil outcomes.

- There is a need for teachers and leaders to understand poverty in their context rather than merely in the context of attainment gaps.

Research 4

Child of the North (2024a)

'An evidence-based plan for addressing poverty with and through education settings'

This report is a collaborative programme of work between the organisations Child of the North, N8 Research Partnership and the Centre for Young Lives. The research report emphasises the need for developing and implementing an evidence-based plan to address child poverty through schools and nurseries, particularly in the most deprived communities in the UK. This is the second report in a year-long series by Child of the North and the Centre for Young Lives, aimed at creating a country that supports all children and young people. Although the research has a focus on the North of England, it features a range of best-practice ideas and examples from across the UK.

Key points

- The report underscores the significant negative impacts of poverty on children's education, health and future employment prospects. It notes that over four million children in the UK live in poverty.

- It highlights that children experiencing persistent disadvantage tend to leave school significantly behind their peers, with only 40 per cent of the most disadvantaged pupils reaching expected attainment levels.

- School leaders across the UK report that they are increasingly addressing the impacts of poverty, such as providing food to hungry pupils.

- The report links child poverty with higher rates of school absence, suggesting that pupils facing poverty are more likely to be persistently absent from school.

- The research showcases initiatives like 'Poverty Proofing© the School Day' and the 'Cost of the School Day', which have demonstrated positive impacts on reducing child poverty within school settings. This is discussed further in Chapter 3.
- The report is helpful for school leaders and teachers wanting to understand the issue of poverty in broader terms and beyond the scope of PP and FSM definitions. It also provides an example of how some schools are working with academic researchers and health professionals to both understand and tackle poverty.

Other useful research

U. R. Wagle, 2008: Wagle provides a multifaceted view of poverty, examining both individual and systemic causes of economic disadvantage. Economic wellbeing and Income: Economic wellbeing depends on whether people have enough income to cover basic needs. Broader perspectives: Some researchers link poverty to a lack of personal resources essential for a good standard of living, such as access to education or healthcare. Social and political factors: Others argue that poverty arises from broader social and political issues that impact wellbeing.

D. Sobel, 2018: In his book *Narrowing the Attainment Gap*, Sobel examines how school leaders can better understand and reduce the attainment gap in the context of their setting. Sobel explores the need for teachers and leaders to place further emphasis on understanding attainment gaps in the context of their own schools and specific cohorts of pupils.

Research takeaways

- FSM and pupil premium are regularly used as proxies, but are not sufficient to understand the scale/complexity of poverty in schools.
- Teachers and leaders need to be clear on what poverty and disadvantage mean in their context.
- Schools need a coherent definition and understanding of poverty in their school(s) as part of their strategy to tackle poverty and disadvantage.

- Poverty needs to be understood in the context of individual schools and communities. There are a range of research reports and best-practice examples of how to do this (see the Child of the North report (2024) cited previously).
- It is important for school leaders and teachers to both understand and tackle poverty. Using the research references previously mentioned and a range of current research reports will help leaders to see how poverty is similar and different to national trends in relation to this issue.
- Poverty impacts learning in classrooms. But it can have other far-reaching impacts, such as on access to healthcare, school absence and future learning prospects.

 Case Study

NEAT Academy Trust – Newcastle Research School

Debi Bailey

Poverty and disadvantage impact learning. This is why it is so important for all adults working in our NEAT schools to understand poverty and the barriers to learning that it creates. We have been deliberate about challenging all leaders, teachers and support staff to think of poverty as something which can impact many of our pupils, not just those pupils eligible for pupil premium or free school meals.

Understanding need

Teachers and leaders work on the principle that the better we know our families in terms of strengths and barriers, the more equipped we are to support them. To support this relational, whole-family approach, we developed a trust mantra:

> *'Know our children well, know our families and community well, know each other well'.*

We have developed a shared language and given priority to actively building better relationships. This includes regularly engaging with families by telephone and in person. It includes pastoral and support staff making regular home visits because we know that coming to the school entrance can be difficult for some families due to transport, low income or managing competing demands such as childcare.

In addition, leaders have developed a framework for stakeholder communication with families, especially those facing need due to different levels of disadvantage. The two main aims of this are to support leaders and teachers in:

- understanding and assessing barriers to learning
- addressing barriers to learning and school.

Understanding and assessing barriers to learning

While we have always been proud of our work with families, there was a period when a lack of strategy around this work led us to be less proactive and more reactive.

A lack of clear criteria or shared language to describe barriers and levels of vulnerability and a lack of understanding of their impact on learning prevented us from effectively deploying what resources we had, and ultimately led to us not working with our families as effectively as we could be.

Our whole Trust strategy now involves using a diagnostic tool that applies a range of criteria to identify pupils who are likely to need additional support. Criteria align to priority areas of vulnerability, including socioeconomic disadvantage, SEND, attendance, behaviour for learning, progress, mental health and physical health.

Addressing barriers to learning and school

Like all schools, NEAT schools make use of a range of resources and tools to help develop interventions for families in need. These include but are not limited to:

- working alongside social care professionals
- early help provision
- making use of the Common Assessment Framework (CAF).

Examples include SEND, attendance, physical and mental health health, and behaviour. (See the online resources for a downloadable version of the NEAT windscreen.)

We then developed criteria to assess the level of need and the consequent impact on learning, ranging from Universal (where no need/barrier is known) to Level 4 (where significant barriers and impact are identified and the pupil may for example be CLA (children looked after) or have complex SEND or significant mental health needs).

Conclusions from our work with families and pupils

Schools are now able to promptly build up a holistic understanding of families. Leaders and teachers are able to map knowledge of the pupils and/or the family and work with them to gain a better understanding of factors, both internal and external, which impact their learning.

When our diagnostic tool demonstrates a need for a particular provision, schools then build in resource where it is lacking, e.g. an in-school counselling service or a speech and language therapist. These do cost money, but the diagnostic tool demonstrates a need for this provision. This can also be useful when applying for external funding, as leaders and teachers are able to readily demonstrate the need and how funding will be used to develop provision for pupils with that need.

Leaders work with all staff to create structured conversation frames to support open conversation with families and pupils. Schools have delivered training to adults to support them in being confident in facilitating these discussions.

Leaders have also developed 'heat maps' as a way of collating more complex information and making it accessible to classroom teachers so they have a better understanding of pupils.

Seating plans have been developed across our schools that contain some of the wider barriers that adults need to be aware of. This supports teachers and support staff in classrooms in promptly identifying need and planning to address specific barriers that exist for key groups of pupils.

Underpinning all of this work around building knowledge of children and families is a focus on effective teaching. We prioritise significant amounts of professional development to support adults in developing strategies for effective learning in classrooms.

At NEAT, we believe effective relationships are key to ensuring the best outcomes for all, but particularly for those pupils and families facing sustained poverty.

Like other contributors to this book, we believe that quality education alone cannot fully address systemic inequalities within communities. And neither can educational inequality be addressed by education alone. Building strong, effective partnerships with families is essential, as it enables us to work together to understand and respond to needs. These relationships ensure that our leaders, educators, and support staff avoid making assumptions about the families we serve. Instead, our actions and interventions are informed by genuine collaboration, grounded in shared understanding, and done with families, not to them.

 Ideas to try

Defining poverty and disadvantage

Begin by ensuring that your school has a clear understanding of what is meant by poverty and disadvantage. The reflective tasks provided at the end of this chapter are designed to support leaders and teachers with this.

In our schools, we define poverty as facing disadvantage, insecurity and daily barriers to learning as a result of financial circumstances. However, it is not just about money and poverty can lead to pupils and families facing marginalisation or feeling isolated. It is arguably too simple a definition for some schools, but we have found that it helps to cohesively frame what our school leaders and teachers mean when we refer to poverty and disadvantage in our communities. Here is an example of a working definition used by some school leaders and teachers.

> *'Poverty encompasses more than just money. It can include a lack of access to essential services such as education, healthcare, good housing and food. It also involves social exclusion and a lack of opportunities, leading to a cycle of disadvantage and marginalisation for many children and their families. Poverty can affect an individual's physical and mental health, educational attainment and overall quality of life. It isn't just about learning in our classrooms.'*

All adults in schools need to have a clear understanding of what a definition of poverty looks like in their own community. Consider how each of the following is used to ensure that this understanding is reinforced across the whole school:

- **Staff meetings and training:** Ensure that a coherent language is used around poverty consistently by all. Ensure that poverty is not only referenced as meaning FSM or pupil premium. This is explored further in the following chapter.

- **Strategic school documentation:** Encourage teachers and leaders to consider broader facets of this definition in whole-school and strategic school documentation. For example, challenge staff to think more broadly than pupil premium or FSM when using seating plans. It might include challenging leaders to have different examples of disadvantage, e.g. how poverty can impact different aspects of a child's life, or exploring how other factors can contribute to barriers faced by children living in poverty (e.g. ethnicity, mental health, SEND).

- **Community awareness:** Ensure that the school community is made aware of local issues that contribute to disadvantage for low-income families. This idea is explored further in subsequent chapters. For example, when local library services near to two of our schools closed, teachers and leaders had to consider how this would impact the access that families had to books. Local intelligence like this is an important part of understanding what disadvantage might mean in local 'real-world' terms. Teachers and leaders had to revise their reading strategy so that families and pupils had better and more timely access to books at the end of the school day and during the school day.

- **Tackle misconceptions:** Find out what misconceptions might exist in school regarding those living in poverty or low-income households. For example, some staff might think that low-income families have low aspirations, and one of the main ways a school can help is to try to raise aspirations for the children from those families. Yet some research (CRFR, 2017; Horgan, 2007) indicates that low aspirations are often incorrectly assumed to be a characteristic of low-income families. You could carry out a staff survey or focus group to find out what adults working in schools understand about poverty. This is examined more closely in Chapter 14 of this book.

Diet walks

Diet walks can be useful in helping leaders and teachers to understand more about how poverty and disadvantage can impact pupil learning.

Identify a group of pupils who face barriers to learning as a result of poverty. Invite teachers and leaders to spend time with the pupils through the breadth of a school day to understand the diet of learning and provision that pupils access. This may have a curriculum or subject focus but should also consider those broader aspects of the school day that impact learning (e.g. breaktime, lunchtime).

This approach has worked best in our schools when it has been adapted to fit alongside existing learning walks. Leaders may want to consider simply adding a thread to existing processes, with a clear lens on targeted groups of pupils whom teachers recognise as facing poverty-related barriers to learning. A practical activity to support with the design and implementation of a diet walk is provided in Chapter 6.

Leaders and teachers may wish to consider these questions as part of the diet walks:

- What practical issues or challenges do all pupils face throughout the day in relation to their learning? (Examples: lack of equipment, busy starts to lessons, having to be organised and think about many things at once…)
- When and where do these appear to be particularly challenging or distracting for pupils?
- What barriers to learning present in different subjects? How do these link to what the teacher(s) recognise as barriers faced by the pupil?
- Which of these barriers are made more complex due to poverty or other facets of disadvantage?
- What is break and lunchtime provision like for the pupil(s)?
- How accessible is food and social time during these times for those pupils who might be most hungry? (This is explored further in Chapter 3.)

Teacher research

Some staff in schools will want to understand the complexity of poverty in more depth. This presents an opportunity for schools to engage with research specifically related to poverty.

In our schools, we facilitate teacher research groups to examine research about poverty and local disadvantage. This strategy is explored further in Chapter 14, which covers engaging with research collaboration. These research opportunities are helpful for creating bespoke professional development for staff, whilst also creating deliberate forums in our schools for teachers to apply and sense-check blogs, research papers and other insights from the profession. They have led to some colleagues choosing to focus on master's and doctoral-level research into these topics.

Social justice

At Tees Valley Education, we have found it helpful to think of the wider concept of social justice as part of our strategy to tackle poverty and disadvantage.

This builds on the strategy of ensuring that schools have a clear definition of poverty and disadvantage. We support this in the following ways:

- **Dedicated area of our website:** This explores our definition of social justice and how we help to address this through our work with pupils, families and the profession. (See 'Links' on page 26.)

- **Signposting support:** This is aimed at families struggling to meet the costs of living and who face other facets of disadvantage (e.g. in-work poverty).

- **Dedicated time in leadership meetings:** In these, we discuss poverty and what additional support might be needed in teams to understand local need.

- **Trauma-informed and teacher-education programmes:** These ensure that we have dedicated adults in schools who understand the needs of those in poverty.

- **Facilitating roundtable events with charities, schools and other community champions:** This enables us better understand local need and share a locally relevant, informed understanding of poverty in our community.

Many of these approaches are explored in greater depth in subsequent chapters.

Chapter takeaways

- Ensure that all adults in school have a clear understanding of what poverty and disadvantage mean in your community.
- Approaches to tackling poverty need to move beyond assumptions about children and families (e.g that children from low-income families all have low aspirations).
- Develop the use of 'diet walks' or other strategies to understand what specific barriers to learning exist for children facing different facets of poverty in the school.
- Engage teachers and leaders in specific research or in sense-checking research that already exists in relation to poverty in your community, region or wider society.
- Develop a charter for social justice and equity for education. This should inform other aspects of strategic school documentation in your school and/or classroom(s).

Recap and Reflective tasks

Recap

Indicate which statements are true or false based on your understanding.	True	False
The pupil premium is the single most important proxy that school leaders should be using to help understand the extent of poverty in a school.		
Research shows that children and families in low-income households have low aspirations regarding education and schooling.		
The impact of poverty and disadvantage on learning is a process, not an event. A long-term view is therefore needed if schools are to tackle it.		

Reflective tasks

Reflective task for leaders and teacher educators
<ul><li>Summarise what you understand by the term 'poverty' and/or 'disadvantage'.</li><li>Consider the strengths and limitations of this definition in the context of your school(s).</li><li>We have provided below an example of a definition used in one of our schools, developed by teachers and school leaders completing this task.</li></ul>*'Poverty encompasses more than just money. It can include a lack of access to essential services such as education, healthcare, good housing and food. It also involves social exclusion and a lack of opportunities, leading to a cycle of disadvantage and marginalisation for many children and their families. Poverty can affect an individual's physical and mental health, educational attainment and overall quality of life. It isn't just about learning in our classrooms.'*

Reflective task for leaders and teacher educators

Leadership reflection
Collaborate with a group of other leaders and/or teacher educators in your school(s). Invite them to each complete the previous activity. Then consider and summarise:

Similarities in our understanding and definition of poverty in school(s)	Differences in our understanding and definition of poverty in school(s)

What are some of the local challenges in your community that are exacerbated by poverty and disadvantage?

Reflective task for teachers and curriculum leaders

- What do you understand by the term 'poverty'?
- How would you summarise to a colleague in school(s) what 'poverty' means?

We have provided below an example of a definition used in one of our schools that was developed by teachers and school leaders completing this task.

'Poverty encompasses more than just money. It can include a lack of access to essential services such as education, healthcare, good housing and food. It also involves social exclusion and lack of opportunities, leading to a cycle of disadvantage and marginalisation for many children and their families. Poverty can affect an individual's physical and mental health, educational attainment, and overall quality of life. It isn't just about learning in our classrooms.'

Understanding poverty in your classroom Look back at your definition of poverty and consider the aspects of research explored in this chapter. You may find it helpful to consider a group of pupils that you know fulfil aspects of the criteria you have considered. Then complete these sections with these pupils in mind.	
How does poverty impact learning in your classroom?	
What are some of the ways in which you are addressing these impacts on learning?	
Whole-class approaches	Individual pupil support strategies
What research has been used to help inform these strategies?	
Internal evidence (e.g. within school)	External evidence (e.g. EEF, research papers)

<table>
<tr><td colspan="2">Based on your reading so far in this book, what additional strategies or ideas do you have for further understanding the ways in which poverty impacts learning and how to tackle it?</td></tr>
<tr><td>Ways I can further understand the reality of poverty in the school(s) I serve:</td><td>Ways I can sense-check my strategies for understanding and tackling poverty in my own classroom(s):</td></tr>
<tr><td>

</td><td></td></tr>
</table>

📖 Further reading

Centre for Research on Families and Relationships (2017) – 'Can we put the "poverty of aspiration" myth to bed now?'

Child of the North (2024a) – 'An evidence-based plan for addressing poverty with and through education settings'

Darton and Strelitz (2003) – *Tackling UK Poverty and Disadvantage in the Twenty-First Century: An Exploration of the Issues*

EEF (2023) – 'The EEF guide to the pupil premium: How to plan, implement, monitor and sustain an effective strategy'

Francis-Devine (2023) – 'Poverty in the UK: Statistics'

Gorard et al. (2021) – 'Assessing the impact of Pupil Premium funding on primary school segregation and attainment'

Horgan (2007) – 'The impact of poverty on young children's experience of school'

Kennedy (2010) – 'Child Poverty Act 2010: A short guide'

Links

Tees Valley Education (2024) Social justice and equity in education charter: www.teesvalleyeducation.co.uk/trust-specialisms/social-justice-equality

NEAT Windscreen in the online resources

2 Professional development
Anna Carter, Julia Kedwards

Chapter summary

Effective teaching is a strong lever for improving academic outcomes and life chances of pupils in poverty. As authors of this chapter, we want to highlight that research suggests that quality professional development has a greater effect on pupil attainment than other interventions schools may consider, such as implementing performance-related pay for teachers or lengthening the school day. However, it is important to note that professional development alone is not enough to tackle poverty and disadvantage in schools. Therefore, in this chapter we explore some of the ways in which effective professional development can be designed to support the development of teachers and other adults working in classrooms. We share how professional development across schools can help to develop pedagogical expertise and support staff to better understand and tackle poverty-related barriers to learning.

 What does the research suggest?

There are vast amounts of research into professional development for teachers and guidance on how to develop teacher expertise in schools. This is explored more fully by other books dedicated to the sole topic of professional development in schools. In this section, we summarise some of the main sources of evidence and literature that have supported leaders at NPAT in their design and delivery of professional development. Teacher and professional development are at the core of our strategy to tackle poverty-related barriers to learning and the goal of our schools is to raise academic attainment for every pupil. It is difficult to find research which specifically covers CPD related to poverty and disadvantage in schools, so we have covered the impacts of CPD in general in this chapter as well.

Research 1

Fletcher-Wood and Zuccollo (2020)

'The effects of high-quality professional development on teachers and pupils: A rapid review and meta-analysis'

The Education Policy Institute (EPI) and Ambition Institute, commissioned by the Wellcome Trust, conducted research to explore the costs and benefits of providing all teachers with 35 hours of high-quality professional development annually. The review was led by Harry Fletcher-Wood, who has extensive experience teaching and leading educational programmes internationally, and by James Zuccollo, the Director for School Workforce at EPI, who specialises in research on the school workforce.

Fletcher-Wood and Zuccollo (2020) present a review of evidence regarding the impact of professional development in schools. The review is helpful as a point of reference for school leaders, particularly those responsible for CPD design and development. The study examines over 50 randomised controlled trials evaluating a range of teacher development programmes, aiming to identify the impact of the CPD on pupil and teacher outcomes.

Key points

Key findings from the report include the following with regard to the value of high-quality CPD for pupils:

- The research review indicates that high-quality professional development can close gaps between what novice and experienced teachers do in the classroom.

- The impact of effective professional development on pupil outcomes compares to the impact of having a teacher with broadly ten years' experience over a new teacher. This is important when considering the impact of classroom teaching for pupils facing poverty-related barriers to learning.

- In contrast to some other interventions that schools might use to ensure that pupils in poverty make progress in school (e.g. the lengthening of the school day to allocate more learning hours, additional tutoring for pupils, revision classes for pupils), high-quality professional development has a greater effect on pupil attainment.

It is important to note that this research explores the value of highly effective professional development more broadly, rather than specifically how it can be used to tackle poverty and disadvantage. However, we have used this as school leaders to help remind teachers and schools of the value of designing and implementating effective professional development to lever greater pupil outcomes. Below are some of the other ways in which this research has been used as part of our strategy for tackling the impact of poverty and disadvantage in classrooms:

- This research suggests that increasing access to high-quality professional development can contribute to greater retention rates for teachers in schools, particularly for Early Career Teachers (ECTs). We have designed professional development with this in mind and to retain our best talent in the workforce. This is built on the belief that too much staff turnover or disruption to consistently good teachers in classrooms is likely to have the greatest impact on pupils facing poverty.

- Effective induction and mentoring can also contribute to the retention of teachers in schools. For some of our schools, we have recognised that the challenge of serving in areas of sustained poverty can be very different to teachers' experiences of working in other areas or regions. So, we have used this research to refine our induction processes to put more emphasis on the retention of teachers.

- The research indicates that professional development can have a greater impact in schools when it receives support from school leadership teams and is designed with busy teacher workload in mind.

Research 2

Education Endowment Foundation (2021)

'Effective professional development'

This report is useful for reminding schools of the impact that teachers have in classrooms. The research is not specific to schools with high levels of poverty or disadvantage, but it does indicate the value of designing effective professional development in schools to improve pupil outcomes. We have found this research helpful for reminding all leaders and teachers in our schools that poorly designed and implemented CPD can be detrimental for teachers, and especially for the outcomes of pupils with poverty-related barriers to learning. It is vital that professional development is designed well and that it draws from an evidence base of what educators know works best from our sector. The EEF report offers some practical and actionable recommendations on how schools can ensure that professional development is impactful.

Key points

- **Focus on the mechanisms:** To help improve pupil outcomes, it is important for school leaders to consider the value of *mechanisms* in the CPD design. The EEF identifies mechanisms as the 'core building blocks of professional development' (2021, p. 8). One example is the value of revisiting previous learning in professional development. We have used this to support professional development leaders in our schools, reiterating to teachers the importance of checking for understanding as part of professional development and of providing regular reading opportunities for teachers to understand about barriers to learning that poverty and disadvantage can create. We have also built time into professional development sessions for teachers to plan how to use strategies that have been presented. This can be helpful for supporting teachers to plan for specific pupils who they recognise are facing poverty-related barriers to learning.

- **Build knowledge and develop teachers:** Leaders should ensure that professional development builds knowledge and that thought is given to the cognitive load on teachers and support staff. At NPAT, we have provided training to leaders of professional development in the science of learning and challenged them to be mindful of introducing too much text or information in sessions. This can be helpful for supporting teachers in understanding a particular strategy in the context of one aspect of a barrier faced by children in poverty – for example, introducing to teachers the concept of cognitive load whilst sharing with teachers how poverty can impact focus or attention for some pupils (see Chapter 6).

- **Embed in practice:** Teacher educators and leaders should be mindful to design professional learning that supports those working in classrooms to embed practice. This may involve organising professional development meetings, where educators can plan how to implement new strategies in their classrooms. It could also include regular monitoring and providing prompts to help teachers deepen their understanding and effectively apply the learning within their specific subjects or teaching phases. At NPAT, we routinely give opportunity for teachers to showcase worked examples of how a strategy has been used to support specific pupils who face poverty-related barriers to learning. This can be useful for helping teachers and support staff understand and embed the strategy in their own classroom contexts.

- **Ensure careful implementation:** It is important for teacher educators and leaders to carefully consider the implementation of professional development and the specific context in which it is delivered. Professional development should align with the strategic needs of the school, and it is essential that the implementation is understood and supported by the school leadership team. For example, in our annual teaching and learning conference at NPAT, we routinely share up-to-date poverty and disadvantage statistics with teachers and leaders. We do this to remind all those working in classrooms of the scale of poverty and how it can impact learning in classrooms. We also work with individual schools to consider what specific barriers to learning pupils in that context face because of poverty or disadvantage. It is important that our teams designing professional development do not simply adopt a one-size-fits-all approach.

Research 3

Timperley et al. (2007)

'Teacher Professional Learning and Development: Best Evidence Synthesis Iteration'

This research is published by the New Zealand Ministry of Education as part of the Iterative Best Evidence Synthesis (BES) Programme. The synthesis focuses on understanding the impact of professional learning opportunities on teaching practices and, consequently, pupil outcomes. The research is part of a broader effort to use evidence-based strategies to enhance educational practices and outcomes, particularly focusing on addressing disparities and underachievement in the New Zealand education system for pupils facing disadvantage and from under-represented groups. However, in our experience, it has some helpful insights for the design and delivery of professional learning in UK schools.

The research cites a range of studies that show the positive impact that professional learning and development opportunities for teachers can have on pupil learning, particularly for pupils facing poverty or other facets of disadvantage. We have noted some of the points from the research that specifically explore aspects of improving teaching and learning for pupils facing poverty-related barriers to learning.

Key points

- In some of the schools featured in the research, the progress made by the lowest-achieving 20 per cent of pupils is particularly noteworthy. These pupils experienced average achievement gains equivalent to an extra three to four years of schooling in one year, which was attributed to a range of factors, including effective professional development.

- The use of external experts, such as researchers, was a common feature in most of the core studies of professional development. This is important as it helps teachers develop new skills and perspectives on their practices, which they likely cannot do alone. Experts must possess both content knowledge and the ability to make this knowledge meaningful and manageable for teachers. At NPAT, we have found it important to involve leading researchers and other professionals to train our teachers in specific areas of understanding poverty. This is explored in more depth in the next section.

- Effective professional development was used by some schools to challenge assumptions about different groups of pupils and their learning abilities, which changed as teachers saw the impact of new approaches to teaching practices on pupil outcomes and learning in the classroom.

- Some of the studies showed how professional development can support teachers to take more responsibility for all pupils' learning, rather than attributing learning difficulties solely to their home or community situations. For instance, a New Zealand study aimed at improving relationships with Māori pupils in secondary schools showed that teachers' actions in classrooms greatly influence how pupils respond to learning in and out of classrooms.

Research takeaways

- Professional development of teachers is a significant lever for change in schools; it demands careful design and implementation if it is to make a difference to the quality of teaching.
- Research continues to indicate the positive impact that professional learning and development opportunities for teachers can have on pupil learning, particularly for pupils facing poverty or other facets

of disadvantage. However, it is important to remember that these studies rarely talk about poverty or disadvantage as a discrete topic, because effective professional learning is likely to lead to a positive impact for all pupils.

- Effective professional development can support with induction, development and retention of staff in schools. This is an important part of securing consistently good practice for pupils in schools that face poverty-related barriers to learning.

- Poverty is multifaceted (as explored in other chapters). So it is important that professional development is designed with context-specific issues in mind. Not every pupil in poverty faces the same barriers. It is important to establish what these are for each pupil and then design professional development with them in mind.

- Professional development can be used to challenge assumptions about groups of pupils and what pupils might be capable of. This is important in schools serving areas of high poverty and disadvantage.

- The use of external experts, such as researchers or health professionals, can support with effective professional learning design and delivery. This might be especially important when focusing on specific barriers to learning caused by poverty or disadvantage (e.g. trauma or health inequality).

 Case Study

Northampton Primary Academy Trust (NPAT)

NPAT comprises 14 primary schools in Northampton, Wellingborough and Milton Keynes. A number of these schools serve areas of high deprivation. Data analysis across the schools in the early years of its inception showed that there were significant gaps between the outcomes of pupils with poverty-related barriers to learning and all other pupils. To explore the educational disadvantage gap in greater depth, leaders at NPAT worked closely with Unity Research school and pupil premium advisor Marc Rowland. A key recommendation from this collaboration was that professional development in NPAT schools should be designed with poverty and disadvantage-related barriers to learning at the forefront. This was also influenced by the earlier research reading we had undertaken, which indicates the value of drawing on external expertise, particularly in relation to complex topics such as poverty and disadvantage.

Professional development expertise

Our first step was to ensure that leaders with a responsibility for professional development at NPAT had a level of expertise to both design and deliver effective professional development. Headteachers and other system leaders in NPAT schools are an integral part of this, and so we spent considerable time ensuring that leaders understood the research about professional development.

Our professional development lead was enrolled onto a national professional development programme with Ambition Institute so that they could understand the principles of effective CPD design. Leadership time was given across schools to help ensure that headteachers and teacher educators had regular opportunity to engage with research and consider how it applied to different school contexts. This helped to develop a consistent language around CPD across NPAT leadership teams and meant that leaders had a consensus of what constitutes high-quality effective professional development. Phrases such as 'teacher educator', 'deliberate practice' and 'instructional coaching' are now part of the everyday language at NPAT schools, and teachers understand these. We do not use them instead of the phrase 'professional development' but alongside it, so that all staff understand what we mean when we talk about professional development in practice.

Ensuring professional development has disadvantage at the core

Every year, NPAT facilitates a teaching and learning conference which brings all of our schools and teacher educators together for collaborative professional development. Examples of themes explored in these day-long conferences include:

- understanding poverty-informed practice
- examining how effective teaching of reading can support pupils with poverty-related barriers to learning
- understanding up-to-date research on poverty statistics in our communities.

We have benefited from inviting keynote speakers as part of these annual conferences, including Marc Rowland, Becky Francis and Sean Harris. Facilitating these conferences helps to consolidate the message from leaders that NPAT schools are committed to understanding how to tackle poverty and disadvantage in schools.

Understanding local poverty and disadvantage

Leaders have worked collaboratively with teachers and support staff in their schools to consider and agree shared definitions of poverty. Professional development time has been dedicated to consider local poverty statistics and specific barriers to learning that exist for pupils that are in poverty or even close to some of these poverty measures. This has helped to ensure that all adults working in NPAT schools have a shared understanding of what leaders mean when they refer to pupils that are vulnerable or pupils that face poverty-related barriers to learning.

Understanding the whole-school response to poverty and disadvantage

Our initial strategic priority was ensuring that teacher educators and leaders in NPAT schools understood some of the complexities of poverty and disadvantage. However, this now spans to all leaders, governance and staff working across our schools. It is important that all staff understand the challenges faced by families and children living in or close to poverty. Teacher educators and leaders in schools use a range of approaches to facilitate this, including:

- regular research roundups distributed to all staff that summarise aspects of up-to-date poverty research and the challenges faced by families nationally and locally
- signposting of support and advice for members of staff and families on dealing with increases in the cost of living and financial hardship
- reminding teachers and leaders of main takeaway points or messages shared as part of NPAT annual teaching and learning conferences
- routine reminders of safeguarding and supporting pupils or families in crisis, recognising that this is the responsibility of every adult (this is explored more extensively in other chapters)
- ensuring that curriculum and lesson planning documentation supports staff to consider careful implementation of teaching strategies

Professional development

- recommending national and regional events that shine a spotlight on aspects of research or themes linked to the disadvantage agenda
- actively encouraging teachers and support staff to identify external training and events that are of interest to them on these themes, and prioritising attendance when possible.

Linking professional development to specific poverty-related barriers to learning

Improving reading ability and access for pupils is a key area of focus for many of our schools, because we have identified this as a specific barrier to learning for many pupils facing poverty and disadvantage in Northampton. Therefore, a CPD programme on the teaching of vocabulary was designed and is delivered to all teaching staff at NPAT. Schools are supported to implement vocabulary strategies in reading initially, broadening to other areas of the curriculum after this. Teacher educators work closely with leaders of reading and English in schools to underpin the teaching of reading in classrooms. Alongside this, a regular series of CPD seminars is used to remind teachers of the science of learning and how children learn. This helps to build a degree of expertise in both reading and in supporting disadvantaged pupils to overcome poverty-related barriers to reading in and out of school.

Induction of new teachers and ECTs in NPAT schools includes a thread on the teaching of vocabulary and on cognitive science. All new staff at NPAT attend an induction session led by the CEO and Trust Lead for professional development. As part of these sessions, the NPAT strategy for understanding and tackling poverty is shared with staff, and colleagues are encouraged to ask questions about this.

Evaluation to inform future developments

We dedicate specific time to our leaders for exploring what is working and what might not be working by way of supporting disadvantaged pupils and families. Our teacher educators are critical to this, because insights from these sessions can be further explored as part of professional development pathways of support for established and emerging leaders across NPAT. Case studies are regularly shared amongst teacher educators and leaders working in our schools, to ensure an emphasis on best practice and to support other schools in understanding how to apply the principles of a given strategy or intervention.

 Ideas to try

Other approaches specific to tackling poverty and disadvantage that we use in our schools include the following:

- **Research roundup:** We use poverty research and up-to-date poverty data to help our workforce understand the scale of poverty and how it impacts families. Much of this is widely available through sources such as the Joseph Rowntree Foundation and Child Poverty Action Group. For example, CPAG's annual Cost of a Child report looks at how much it costs families to provide a minimum socially acceptable standard of living for their children. It is calculated using the Minimum Income Standard (MIS) research, carried out by the Centre for Research in Social Policy at Loughborough University for the Joseph Rowntree Foundation. The UK Poverty from JRF reports use a range of data sources and insights to build up a comprehensive picture of the current state of poverty across the UK. As poverty can lead to negative impacts at all stages of life, these regular reports help tell the narrative of who is worst affected, how levels have changed over time and what the future prospects might be.

- **Induction:** As part of induction, we dedicate time to helping teachers and leaders understand specific barriers to learning that leaders know are amplified because of poverty or disadvantage. This is helpful for illustrating to new teachers the scale of challenges in classrooms, but for also addressing any misconceptions the staff member may have because they have worked in areas/schools with less pronounced levels of disadvantage.

- **Showcase best practice:** We ensure that teachers and support staff have the opportunity in professional learning sessions to showcase specific strategies and how these are used with specific pupils facing poverty. This can be helpful for supporting teachers to embed strategies and reminding staff about specific poverty-related barriers to learning faced by key pupils.

Professional development

Chapter takeaways

- Develop a strong knowledge base in your school/trust regarding effective professional development and why this is important for tackling poverty-related barriers to learning.
- Prioritise developing understanding of how children and adults learn.
- Ensure that professional development has the topics of poverty and disadvantage at the core. Whilst good teaching will Impact all pupils, it is especially important for vulnerable groups of pupils and those facing specific facets of disadvantage.
- Draw on external expertise that might be needed to help leaders and teachers understand complex issues faced by pupils and families living in sustained poverty. This will help busy teachers and leaders working in schools in areas of pronounced disadvantage.
- Recognise that sustainable school improvement takes time and should be planned carefully. The updated EEF (2024) school implementation guide is a good example of how school leaders can achieve this.

Recap and Reflective tasks

Recap

Indicate which statements are true or false based on your understanding.	True	False
High-quality professional development can have a more significant impact on pupil attainment than many other school interventions, such as extending the school day.		
During professional development programmes, it is useful to showcase specific strategies teachers in the school have implemented and evaluated.		
Research indicates that even high-quality and effective professional development is unlikely to impact outcomes for pupils living in the most disadvantaged of contexts.		
Recent research indicates that high-quality professional development programmes have the potential to close gaps between novice and experienced teachers in the classroom.		

Reflective tasks

Reflective task for leaders and teacher educators
How would you define what professional development opportunities exist in your school(s)? Write a summary definition of how professional development is used as part of the strategy for tackling poverty-related barriers to learning.

Further reflection

Considering this definition, identify a specific strand or type of professional learning currently offered in your school(s) to address an aspect of poverty/disadvantage.

Aims and intent	Barriers to learning
What issue or area of need is the professional development seeking to address? How do you know that this is an issue?	Consider the barriers to learning that this professional development is seeking to address.

What knowledge of poverty and disadvantage do you want teachers to understand?

What prior learning can you draw on to support teachers in understanding this?

What credible sources or external expertise might you need to draw on to support teacher understanding in your school(s) about this?

What specific strategies or teaching techniques will you support teachers' use of to improve teaching practice?

How will the professional development support teachers to embed this practice for pupils facing specific poverty-related barriers to learning? E.g. provide action-planning time, further monitoring, collaborative planning in teams, and so on.

Reflective task for teachers/curriculum leaders

- Identify and think back to some recent professional development you received in or out of your school context.
- Use this review section to consider how it relates to aspects of poverty-informed practice and how you can further embed this in your classroom/team.

Summarise what the professional development was about and the main points that it covered.

Next, consider some specific poverty-related barriers to learning that you believe that this professional development might help to address in the context of your classroom.

Poverty-related barriers to learning:

What will I action because of this learning and in relation to these barriers?	What impact do I want these actions to have in relation to my classroom?

Once you have trialled the strategy/action, reflect on the next questions with a colleague.

How did pupils respond? What do we think was the initial impact?	What might we need to do differently next time to further address the poverty-related barriers to learning?

Next, use this reflection to further support your ongoing development and to facilitate a discussion with your team/line manager regarding next steps.

Further learning that I would like to engage in following my reading of this chapter and/or since trialling some of the actions outlined:

Other aspects of poverty and disadvantage that I am interested in exploring more about as part of my continuing professional development:

Make a note of ideas or reflections for where you could further access this support and development opportunities.

📖 Further reading

Darling-Hammond et al. (2017) – *Effective Teacher Professional Development*
EEF (2024) – 'A school's guide to implementation: Guidance report'
Guskey (2002) – 'Professional development and teacher change'
Harris (2022) – 'Poverty on the brain: Five strategies to counter the impact of disadvantage'
Rowland (2021) – *Addressing Educational Disadvantage in Schools and Colleges: The Essex Way*
Timperley et al. (2007) – *Teacher Professional Learning and Development: Best Evidence Synthesis*

Links

EEF – Effective professional development resources:
https://educationendowmentfoundation.org.uk/education-evidence/guidance-reports/effective-professional-development
CPAG – Reports on the cost of a child: https://cpag.org.uk/news/cost-child-2024
JRF – Reports on UK poverty: https://www.jrf.org.uk/uk-poverty-2024-the-essential-guide-to-understanding-poverty-in-the-uk

3 Poverty Proofing© the School Day

Lorna Nicoll, Luke Bramhall

Chapter summary

In this chapter, we explore Poverty Proofing© the School Day, an approach used by schools across the UK to be poverty-informed and to address poverty-related barriers to school across multiple areas of school life. In this chapter, we focus on some of the broad themes that have emerged from implementing the Poverty Proofing the School Day project with a wide range of schools (e.g. addressing food poverty, the cost of uniform and access to curriculum resources).

 What does the research suggest?

Identifying poverty-related barriers to school and to learning and then taking actions to address these barriers is an effective approach to tackling poverty and educational disadvantage. The Poverty Proofing the School Day approach is an effective way to do this.

Children North East

Children North East (CNE)

Background

In 2011, CNE gave 1,000 children cameras and asked them to take photographs of what poverty looked like through their eyes. The aim of this research was to support the charity in better understanding how to support those who are impacted by poverty. Children submitted over 11,000 photographs.

CNE then spent a year working with four schools in the North East of England, talking directly to pupils, asking about their experience of school and what it is like facing poverty. CNE heard hundreds of experiences of children whose school day was impacted as a consequence of financial insecurity.

Common themes through the research included:

- **FSM and stigmatising:** Other pupils were aware of who was eligible for FSM through structures existing in school, e.g. FSM codes in the register and having different-coloured exercise books.
- **Visits and FSM food:** Some pupils experienced further shame when participating in offsite visits when having to access their FSM by receiving a paper lunch bag.
- **Access to FSM food:** Some secondary schools did not allow those eligible for FSM to access their food allowance at breaktimes, even though that is when peers would access food. This left pupils in a difficult situation, where they had to make choices of either not spending time with their friends or remaining hungry and having to avoid socialising in canteen spaces.
- **Extra-curricular activities and trips:** Children and families talked about barriers of costs associated with extra-curricular provision and trips. This is not as straightforward as it simply being unachievable to go on a ski trip or a trip to the theme park. CNE heard stories of children not going to the free ballet class because everyone else spent £10 on a tutu, or not going to the paid-for trip to a local attraction because all their peers would take spending money and they didn't want the shame of having to stand outside the shop or sit on the bus home without a souvenir.
- **Rewards and sanctions:** Pupils talked about receiving negative behaviour points because they were unable to complete some homework due to a lack of resources at home, e.g. making a volcano as part of a geography project or a castle as part of a history project.
- **Hidden costs:** Pupils and families shared feeling pressures of costs for buying teacher presents and bringing in a cake for the child's birthday.

Poverty Proofing the School Day

It was from this learning that the 'Poverty Proofing the School Day' audit evolved. The aim is to identify and tackle poverty-related barriers to learning. The audit consists of a whole-school evaluation, a written report, an action plan and training for staff and governors. This is aimed at understanding and tackling poverty at scale across the school.

The process involves speaking to every pupil within a school through focus groups and engaging with staff and families to help understand the true extent of the realities through a lens of the whole community. It looks at communication processes, behaviour systems and other whole-school approaches to help understand what the school day is like for the most disadvantaged of pupils and families.

At the end of the process, an audit report is shared with the school leadership team. This is used to support each school to make sense of the findings and consider and prioritise the strategic actions that are needed to address areas of need.

Poverty Proofing the School Day audits can be challenging but highly effective, delivering to the school a rare opportunity to give voice to its most disadvantaged pupils and their families and see their practices through the eyes of all pupils and the wider community.

Research 1

Mazzoli-Smith and Todd (2016)

'Poverty Proofing the School Day: Evaluation and development report'

This research report highlights some of the benefits of the Poverty Proofing the School Day programme. It indicates that there is evidence of impact in many different types of school, including improved attendance and attainment, greater take-up of free school meals, more effective use of pupil premium funding, a less costly school day and an increase in the uptake of school trips and music tuition by disadvantaged pupils.

Key points

- The audit is challenging but highly effective, delivering to the school a rare opportunity to give voice to its most disadvantaged pupils and their families and see their practices through the eyes of all pupils, families and staff.

- There are numerous benefits for the school as a result of going through this process, including a shift in whole-school ethos and culture and the opportunity to make changes in response to the action plan, with maximum impact on pupils.

- The audit provides a constructive opportunity to review pupil premium spending and, through this and other actions, reduce the cost of the school day for pupils in real terms.

- These impacts are dependent on the third-party nature of the audit. Whilst it is very important to share good practice in this area, it is unlikely that the same benefits will be derived if a school reviews these issues in isolation through a self-evaluation process.

- Whole-school buy-in, including from leadership and the academy trust or local authority, is crucial.

Research 2

Beeson et al. (2024)

'Does tackling poverty-related barriers to education improve school outcomes? Evidence from the North East of England'

This research was conducted by Beeson et al. (2024) and focused on the impact of the Poverty Proofing programmes on improving school outcomes, particularly for pupils facing poverty and disadvantage. The study analysed the effects of Poverty Proofing in 38 primary schools in the North East of England, compared to 292 other primary schools in the region.

Key points

- The results showed that when schools took action to address poverty-related barriers, educational outcomes improved for all pupils, with scores increasing by approximately five per cent over a two-year period.

- Removing poverty-related barriers to education can lead to improvements in school outcomes, including average grades and progress. This can be achieved through making use of the Poverty Proofing the School Day initiative in schools.

- Analyses of pupils receiving FSM and those not receiving FSM suggest that the entire school benefits from addressing poverty-related barriers, not just the pupils potentially most affected by poverty. This builds on earlier ideas explored in Chapter 1 of this book. The findings indicated a possible enhancement in learning engagement due to fewer disruptions linked to poverty-related issues.

- Even considering potential sample selection biases, the results indicate that when school leaders prioritise addressing poverty-related learning obstacles, they can enhance school outcomes for all pupils.

 Ideas to try

The Poverty Proofing the School Day approach is based on a tested model that is used consistently across hundreds of schools, but the outputs and findings of the approach will of course vary with individual school contexts. Through understanding the lived experience of those experiencing poverty, the Poverty Proofing team and schools have been able to identify and remove many of the systemic and structural barriers. Below, we have provided some of the broad and consistent themes that have surfaced from using the Poverty Proofing the School Day approach with a wide range of schools across the UK.

Food

This is a vital area of need that includes access to food and the administration of paid and FSM provision.

Barriers

- **Accessing food:** Some pupils may be coming into school hungry and/or do not have enough food to sustain them. Lunchtime portion sizes may be too small and pupils are often unable to get seconds or don't get the food choices they need because of lunchtime queues or duration.
- **Affordability of food:** This is an increasingly common barrier for families and pupils in secondary schools, who frequently report that they have to

choose between having enough to eat or having drinks that cost money (e.g. juice or hot drinks).

- **Administration:** Not all pupils who should be entitled to FSM are being registered. This may be due to online applications, administration charges for schools for each application received or the stigma attached to eligibility.

- **Access to funds:** In some secondary schools, eligible pupils may be unable to access their funds before lunchtime or unable to roll over unspent allowance.

- **Dinner debt:** This is a sensitive area. Pupils involved in taking letters home about it feel embarrassed or stigmatised.

- **Environment:** Some pupils find the designated eating areas challenging. Areas can be noisy, messy and rushed. Food choices can be made based on where pupils are allowed to sit, such as packed lunches together, and some pupils eligible for FSM do not take up their eligibility based on this.

Suggestions

- Consider ways of offering enough food at all points in the day, e.g. some schools work with external partners to provide breakfast; others provide food items such as cereal bars to help pupils at break, in addition to the universal offer of fruit to young children.

- In one of our partner schools, emphasis has been put on having a restaurant-type experience, with pre-laid round tables where pupils are encouraged to participate in discussion. The head cook knows children by name and there is little restriction on the combination of food and how much is offered to each child. The atmosphere is calm and the emphasis is on quiet, sociable eating. Teachers are encouraged to eat in the dinner hall with pupils.

- Be clear about costs but have systems in place for discreet and supportive debt collection.

- Support families to apply for FSM and ensure that it is not possible to identify who is in receipt of them.

- Establish a calm environment in the dinner hall that is supportive of all pupils.

Uniform

Pupils and families have often shared with our researchers that uniform is a positive way to promote inclusion and not highlight those who are struggling financially, but barriers still exist to this.

Barriers

- **Affordability of school essentials:** Uniform policies lead to unintended consequences based on financial background. There is a difference between disobeying rules and not being able to afford uniform. For example, a school may implement a renewed approach to uniform standards and insist on a particular type of footwear instead of trainers. However, if this is done with limited notice or requires families shopping beyond local supermarkets, then it will create additional pressures and financial strains for families with low income. Certain periods of the year may be more difficult for low-income families to maintain correct or adequate footwear. For example, in winter, footwear may become damaged or be difficult for pupils walking or travelling long distances. In one school, pupils told us that they were unable to store footwear at school or in classrooms that they could have changed into after arriving at school in more affordable footwear that is adequate for wintery conditions.

- **Pre-loved:** Many schools have set up schemes to promote used uniform; however, this can cause barriers in itself. In some communities, there is a lot of stigma attached to second-hand clothes.

Suggestions

- Reduce the cost of uniform by removing expensive and unnecessary uniform items, e.g. consider the cost of logos through offering sew- or iron-on labels or removing them altogether and offering discreet support where required.

- Allow families time to buy replacement items such as shoes, rather than expecting them to be purchased straight away.

- When setting up pre-loved schemes, promote sharing of outgrown clothes as a positive way to move forwards.

- Involve other partners such as community centres and food banks to distribute used uniform, e.g. all new pupils in one secondary school we have worked with receive a blazer at no cost, which can then be swapped for another one once they have grown out of it. This is organised through a local charity but in partnership with the school, to ensure that the right resources are allocated to families in the most need.

- Involve pupils and emphasise the environmental outcomes. Monitor the take-up of used uniform to determine how effective it is.

School costs

Schools work hard to remove costs associated with learning. However, our work has shown that this continues to be a significant barrier for many pupils.

Barriers

- **Resources:** Pupils can find it stigmatising when they don't have the required resources, e.g. not having a scientific calculator for homework or feeling that they would achieve more if they could afford a revision guide. They have also spoken of feeling embarrassed when support is provided publicly, e.g. going to the front of the class to receive ingredients for food technology.

- **Trips:** Extra-curricular activities put additional strains on school budgets, and costs are sometimes transferred to families. Excursions and residential trips are costly and there are children who have never experienced one at any point in their school careers. Often, children and young people have expressed feeling different, even stigmatised, when faced with this.

- **Hidden costs:** Families are faced with many unexpected costs at schools, e.g. specialised clothes or equipment. Extra-curricular clubs can also come with upfront or hidden costs, which may deter or prevent pupils from attending, e.g. they do not want to be the only ones in their PE kit when everyone else is in the latest football strip, or travel to and from clubs can cause difficulties if they are after school.

- **Homework and out-of-school resources:** Many families have difficulties with access to the internet and devices for homework that is provided online by schools. Homework requiring resources like money or help from adults or older siblings, such as model-making or virtual creation (e.g. video editing), can strain family finances. Some secondary school pupils have said they have less time for homework because they need to work paid jobs to support their families. This has been especially the case for sixth form pupils we have worked with.

Suggestions

- Provide all resources for the curriculum, including homework. In one Welsh secondary school that we work with, teachers make use of resource boxes in classrooms. Pens, pencils and rulers, amongst other resources, are provided. Pupils take what they need at the beginning of the lessons and replace it at the end of lessons. As well as ensuring that everyone is properly equipped, it has reduced the amount of low-level disruption and increased learning time.
- If it is necessary to bring items in from home, ensure that there are systems to provide discreet support.
- Introduce measures to ensure accessibility of school trips and clubs to all. Monitor the take-up to see who participates fully in school life, and assess whether these measures are effective for ensuring proportional representation of disadvantaged pupils.
- Ensure curriculum/phase leaders and classroom teachers understand the hidden curriculum costs that may exist in their specific subject or phase areas. (The tasks provided at the end of this chapter support with this.)

Support for families

Schools play a vital role within society, and families have consistently told us that they value this. Many schools work relentlessly in their messaging to reach out to families in need and to make it known that help is available. However, sometimes barriers will prevail over this message.

Barriers

- Families often feel uncomfortable asking for financial support.
- High staff turnover and pressures in personal life can impact ongoing relationships between schools and families.

Suggestions

- Work with school staff to increase their understanding and knowledge of how lived experiences of poverty can positively affect relationships with families experiencing poverty.
- Language is everything. Being careful not to 'other' those living in poverty, through school communications and encounters with families, is crucial to the inclusion agenda.

- Produce an annual calendar of events for families that outlines all cost implications.
- Signpost regularly to external agencies. Local authorities and charities can support by providing this information and keeping it up to date.

Chapter takeaways

- Schools need to regularly check what the cost and experience of the school day is like for pupils facing poverty and disadvantage.
- Provide all resources for classroom learning and homework to help deliver an inclusive curriculum.
- Ensure that uniform policies are well implemented so that they do not contribute to financial strain for low-income families.
- Equitable access to food is vital. Check that policies and procedures support access to food for all pupils, but especially those facing poverty-related barriers to learning.
- Consider making use of the Poverty Proofing the School Day audit to both identify and develop strategies for tackling poverty and disadvantage across the whole school community.

⊞ Recap and Reflective tasks

Recap

Indicate which statements are true or false based on your understanding.	True	False
Taking an approach such as Poverty Proofing the School Day is a one-off event and is only beneficial for schools early on in formulating their strategy for tackling poverty.		
Schools need to routinely understand what the cost and experience of the school day is like for those with lived experience of poverty and disadvantage.		
Families have commonly shared that they feel uncomfortable asking for financial support from schools.		

Reflective tasks

Reflective task for all readers
• Summarise in a few sentences your main takeaways from this chapter.
• What questions do you have about the experience of the school day for pupils facing poverty in your own context?
Understanding the cost of schools Consider completing this reflection independently and then collaborate with another teacher/leader to consider how your insights are different.

How much does it cost for a pupil to come to your school throughout the year?
You may find this helpful to complete around a specific year group/phase.

Consider approximate costings of:

Food

Uniform

Additional resources (give examples)

Trips/excursions

Homework/out-of-class learning (e.g. revision)

<table>
<table>
<tr><td>Accessibility and additional support
Summarise some of the additional layers of support that are used in school to support pupils and families facing poverty.</td><td>Communicating this support
Next, consider the ways in which this support is routinely communicated to pupils/families.</td></tr>
</table>
</table>

Experiencing the school day
Complete this reflection initially with other colleagues and then consider working with a group of pupils/families to better consider how this compares and contrasts to their own experience.

Which aspects of the school day do you think would be most difficult for pupils from low-income backgrounds?
(It is important that this reflection is not implemented in a way that will add to any stigma or feeling of isolation for these pupils. So, consider sharing this with all pupils and inviting confidential feedback, e.g. via a survey.)

School perceptions
(e.g. teachers, leaders, support staff)

Pupil perceptions
Family/parental perceptions

📖 Further reading

Beeson et al. (2024) – 'Does tackling poverty related barriers to education improve school outcomes? Evidence from the North East of England'

Mazzoli-Smith and Todd (2019) – 'Conceptualising poverty as a barrier to learning through "Poverty proofing the school day": The genesis and impacts of stigmatisation'

Ridge (2002) – *Childhood Poverty and Social Exclusion: From a Child's Perspective*

Ridge (2011) – 'The everyday cost of poverty in childhood: A review of qualitative research exploring the lives and experiences of low-income children in the UK'

Wikeley et al. (2007) – 'Educational relationships outside school: Why access is important'

Links

Children North East:
https://children-ne.org.uk/what-is-poverty-proofing-the-school-day

4 Early help and intervention
Laura McPhee

Chapter summary

Early help is the name for services that support children and families before they meet the statutory threshold for intervention from children's social care. These services can include parenting support, playgroups and intensive services like counselling and disability support. Schools are uniquely placed to identify concerns early, provide help for children and prevent concerns from escalating. This chapter explores how a high-quality early help offer can fundamentally transform life outcomes for pupils.

 What does the research suggest?

The importance of early help and multi-agency working to support families and children facing poverty is well documented. In this section, I signpost some of the specific research and literature that has supported my own work as a headteacher and that of colleagues working in busy school environments. This research has been helpful in understanding the importance of early help and how to implement it with families.

Research 1
Bywaters et al. (2020)
'The Child Welfare Inequalities Project: Final report'
The Child Welfare Inequalities Project (CWIP) aimed to highlight and address inequalities in child welfare systems in the UK and around the world. The project focused on understanding why some children and families are more likely to need social welfare services based on where they live, their age and other factors. The research also explored how family situations and the way services respond to them create these inequalities. For this reason, it is helpful for understanding why early help is vital.

Key points

The CWIP research indicates why early help is needed for many children and families that face poverty and inequality. For example:

- Children in the most deprived ten per cent of small neighbourhoods in the UK are more likely to be in foster care or residential care or on protection plans compared to children in the least deprived ten per cent.
- Approximately 55 per cent of children on protection plans or in state care originate from the most deprived 20 per cent of neighbourhoods.
- This contrasts with 45 per cent of children who come from the less deprived 80 per cent of neighbourhoods.

Research 2

Buttle UK (2023)

'The State of Child Poverty 2023: Exploring the changing face of child poverty in a cost-of-living crisis'

Buttle UK is a charity that supports children and young people in crisis across the UK, in particular those living in financial hardship and dealing with challenging social issues. In recent years, the charity has produced an annual research report to demonstrate the reality of child poverty in the UK and the lived experience of millions of children and families facing financial hardship. Respondents to the State of Child Poverty survey 2023 were asked about adverse childhood experiences in the home.

Key points

A significant portion of families surveyed reported financial hardships. Examples included:

- 57 per cent struggled to afford enough food and nutrition.
- Almost 60 per cent were unable to afford utilities (e.g. gas, electricity).
- Almost 50 per cent had difficulties with paying rent or housing costs.

These financial hardships create further difficulties and inequalities for these households, leading to increased trauma and adverse childhood experiences. Severe examples included mental health challenges in 70 per cent of the households and neglect being present in 55 per cent of the households.

- The research shows that a lack of basic necessities has contributed to a mental health crisis amongst children and young people. This crisis is linked to poorer educational outcomes and increased school absenteeism. Mental health issues often go untreated or are addressed too late, leading to long-term impacts and escalating family problems. Children in these situations can feel isolated and struggle to build relationships and access opportunities outside their homes. This further reinforces the need for early help for children and families facing these situations.

- Effective early help can help to identify significant and emerging barriers to learning. This in turn will support schools and other professionals in helping to ensure that learning, where possible, is less disrupted and that both children and families can be supported.

Other useful research

- **Action for Children (2022):** This introduces the concept of a preventative ratio, a measure they use to determine the proportion of children receiving early intervention support. According to this research, for every two children who receive early help, there can be an additional three children in social care.

- **Davis and Marsh (2020):** This explores the way in which intersectionality can result in multiple forms of discrimination. Intersectionality is the idea that different aspects of our identity (e.g. gender, race, class) can multiply to increase social exclusion. Families can experience discrimination differently according to their overlapping identities. This is important, as schools will want to understand the lived experiences within their communities.

- **Joseph Rowntree Foundation (2022):** This indicates that poverty rates can be significantly higher in households with both disabled adults and children, more than twice as high compared to families without any disabled family members. This shows the importance for school leaders to recognise the broader complex challenges faced by families facing poverty and disadvantage when developing early help support.

Research takeaways

- Early help is the name for services that support children and families before they meet the (statutory) threshold for intervention from children's social care.
- When pupils and families are marginalised by financial hardship, the trauma they experience can be increased by the circumstances they are required to endure.
- It is important for school leaders and teachers to understand that poverty and disadvantage are multifaceted, and this makes them arguably more complex than many of the other challenges that schools face.
- Poverty is neither a necessary factor in the occurrence of child abuse and neglect, nor a determining factor. However, there are links that need to be sensitively understood by schools.

 Case Study

Loughborough Primary School – early help

Loughborough Primary School developed a pilot that sought to tackle poverty through effective early help and intervention. The school also works alongside Lambeth's Early Help Strategic Group, supporting colleagues across the borough to implement a partnership-wide Early Help Strategy.

Access to data

The partnership with Lambeth's Early Help Strategic Group has enabled the school to access local data, which is used to inform provision. For example, if there are increases in the proportion of pupils on a Child in Need Plan who are accessing support for domestic violence, leaders and teachers 'look upstream' and investigate what support can be put in place for the community at an earlier stage.

This has resulted in earlier signposting to third parties and charities and compulsory training for staff and governors.

Principles of an early help schools-based offer

The designated safeguarding leads (DSLs) set four key principles underlying the school's early help offer. The aim is to develop a sustainable, comprehensive offer that meets these objectives over time and reflects Maslow's principles (see page 62).

- Ensure there is parity, equity and equality of opportunity for pupils, families and the wider community.
- Improve the health and wellbeing of the wider school community.
- Ensure our pupils and school community have every opportunity to be successful.
- Ensure families have access to early intervention that is aligned to their wants, needs and goals.

The DSLs carried out an extensive consultation with a range of stakeholders, including families, teaching and support staff, community police officers, health teams, the local authority PSHE (personal, social, health and economic) lead and specialist practitioners (including the advice and expertise of the local authority's early help working party). The school made improvements to the early help offer based on feedback from the consultation.

Social and self-esteem needs

Parents provided school leaders with detailed feedback about how they would like to see social and self-esteem needs developed. Reduced funding for outreach and community programmes during the cost-of-living crisis led to an increase in demand and a lack of supply. As a result, the school extended its wrap-around offer and now works more closely with children's centres and local charities such as BLAM (Black Learning Achievement Mental Health), which delivers curriculum projects to Key Stage 2 pupils. BLAM promotes positive narratives for pupils of global majority heritage and provides additional services, including free racial wellness therapy and an advocacy service for parents of Black British pupils who need representation after exclusion.

Monitoring and challenge

The school's early help support is closely monitored by a safeguarding governor and the Quality of Education Committee. The local authority DSL lead is also available to advise and support. All staff recognise that open dialogue and a high level of supportive challenge is required.

Evaluating success

In 2023, 62 per cent of the families who requested support received help with housing. Overall, 56.25 per cent received legal support, 50 per cent received advice and guidance and 43.75 per cent of this group also had a child who was receiving counselling at school. The categories of need for support are in line with the locality data received from the local authority, and therefore indicate that we have been successful at implementing support at an earlier stage. At the end of the first year of the project, strengths and difficulties questionnaires indicated that 76 per cent of pupils in receipt of support demonstrated improvement in their total difficulties, 42 per cent saw an improvement in hyperactivity, 42 per cent demonstrated improvement with relationships with peers and 68 per cent demonstrated an improvement with social skills.

 Ideas to try

Maslow's hierarchy of needs

The school framework is based on the principles of Maslow's hierarchy of needs (1943), a motivational theory in psychology comprising a five-tier model of human need. As school leaders, we have found it helpful to consider needs as overlapping circles rather than the traditional hierarchical pyramid (see Figure 1).

Maslow's hierarchy of needs model is helpful for school leaders as it provides a structured framework for understanding and addressing pupils' different needs. By placing needs into five levels – physiological, safety, belongingness, esteem and self-actualisation – the model helps school leaders prioritise interventions and support services effectively.

For instance, ensuring pupils have access to nutritious meals and a safe learning environment (physiological and safety needs) can enhance their ability to focus on tasks in classrooms. Addressing pupils' social and emotional needs (belonging and esteem) through supportive relationships and recognition can foster a positive school or classroom environment.

School leaders or teachers unfamiliar with this approach may find it helpful to adopt the model below from our school to help map strategies to meet the foundational needs of pupils.

Two differing ways to consider a hierarchy of needs

Maslow's hierarchy of needs

Overlapping needs

Consultation and collaboration

Loughborough Primary School has a high level of contact with pupils, but as this is limited to the school day and setting, it can lead to a one-dimensional perspective of pupil experience.

Suggestions

- Lean on other highly skilled professionals from the school's network and invite them to critically evaluate the early help offer.
- Ensure a range of expertise is represented, including health and social care and, where appropriate, youth offending teams, safety schools' officers and community groups.
- Create opportunity for governors and trustees to get involved so that they have the opportunity to contribute and so that they have sufficient subject knowledge to hold leaders to account at a later date.
- Remember to include the pupils and families as the main stakeholders.
- Use data and evidence to understand need and impact of interventions. This should include a blend of quantitative and qualitative data (e.g. pupil attendance data but also comments from families/pupils about how the

intervention might have supported their attendance). It is important to layer data with other forms of intelligence that exist about the realities facing the community and those facing poverty or forms of disadvantage.

Person-centred care

Health professionals explained to us that people might have times when they feel better, followed by times when their symptoms get worse. When healthcare teams set ambitious targets, like strict treatment goals or expected outcomes, there is a risk of missing key information about an individual's circumstances. There is a need for ongoing conversations and offering flexible care.

Suggestions

- **Health provision:** Work with local health authorities and providers to explore whether routine healthcare advice can be provided around school time. This can create opportunities for parents to check in with health professionals.
- **Health advice:** Signpost where families can access health services and health advice through school communications (e.g. the school magazine, website or social media).
- **Ongoing discussions:** For families and individuals dealing with mental health issues, having open conversations means they can keep checking how things are going. Regular opportunities for coffee mornings and family drop-ins can be a useful part of this.
- **Co-production projects:** Co-production with children and families refers to a collaborative approach where professionals, schools and policymakers work together with children and their families to design, deliver and evaluate services and interventions. It recognises that both professionals and families have unique expertise and perspectives that are valuable in creating effective solutions and supporting children's development and wellbeing. Practical approaches to this in the context of research projects are explored in Chapter 14.

Establish a culture of high support and high challenge

To establish a successful early help offer, we have sought to listen to a diverse range of voices and nurture a culture of high support and high challenge. This was helpful in ensuring that school leaders and other colleagues in school had an understanding of early help and which families needed it most. It also helped to ensure that multi-disciplinary teams and professionals from other settings worked closely with school staff to identify which families were in most need. As a result, support and early help could be enacted more promptly for the families and children that would benefit most. Practical approaches to developing this are provided below.

Suggestions

- **Pupil advocacy:** It can be useful for trustees and governors to hear directly from young people on key issues. A committee of pupils who explore high-priority themes and provide feedback to leadership teams can prove invaluable. A list of carefully curated and open-ended questions can offer leadership teams insight into the challenges young people are facing in real time, rather than relying on outdated or perceived barriers.

- **Use of working parties:** Leaders at all levels, teachers and support staff view the school through a distinct lens. When developing initiatives or exploring new ideas, working parties made up of a cross-section of team members can provoke great discourse. They can also be a useful vehicle for more introverted members of the team who are highly skilled and want to contribute.

- **Open-door policy:** Not all conversations need an agenda or a formal meeting. Schools are busy places, with teachers and leaders managing competing priorities. Sometimes the most helpful ideas come along at the most unexpected times. Develop an 'open-door policy' for leaders. This gives all adults the freedom to share their thoughts.

- **Structuring meetings:** Numerous industries within the private sector invite challenge and promote diversity of thought through the structure of their meetings. Try sharing feedback in writing and appointing a spokesperson to share the feedback to encourage honest dissent and avoid the same voices dominating meetings. Trial rotating the chair and introducing ten minutes' quiet reading of any associated papers at the start of the meeting; this allows team members uninterrupted time to formulate their own thoughts before learning the opinions of others.

Chapter takeaways

- Person-centred care and support are important. Support should be done with and not to, especially for those facing real-life barriers as a result of poverty and disadvantage.
- Use data and evidence to understand need and impact of interventions.
- Quality assure support, review regularly and set up systems that provide a high level of scrutiny (for example through governance, internal monitoring, external peer review).

⚙ Recap and Reflective tasks

Recap

Indicate which statements are true or false based on your understanding.	True	False
Schools have a high level of contact with pupils, but as this is limited to the school day and setting it can lead to a one-dimensional perspective of pupil experience.		
Maslow's principles are based on a five-tier model of human needs: physiological, safety, social, self-esteem and self-actualisation.		
Effective early help offers reflect the needs of the locality and context.		
Only quantitative data will give schools the most accurate and current view of which families or pupils need early help intervention.		

The activities provided in this chapter have been provided to primarily support school leaders and those responsible for directing multiple interventions for families in need. However, teachers and other adults wanting to understand more about these approaches may find it helpful to work through these activities with a school leader, pastoral support staff member or SENDCo in their school.

Reflective tasks

Reflective task for school leaders
Reflect on your reading of this chapter, while bearing in mind your understanding of poverty from Chapter 1. Consider your own school context and any other agencies that you have perhaps worked alongside. • In an educational setting, how can we identify which families and children will benefit most from early help intervention?

- Based on your knowledge of your own school and reading of this chapter, how can poverty or aspects of disadvantage compound some of the barriers being faced by these families/pupils?

- In your school/setting, how can professionals collaborate to deepen their understanding of the effects of poverty on care-givers?

<u>Practical application task</u>

This reflection is intended to help you summarise the early help provision offered in your school(s). It maps out the early help provision based on the principles of Maslow's hierarchy of the needs that are present in your school. Use the reflection to consider how your school supports pupils across various levels of need, from basics like safety and belonging to higher-level needs such as learning and personal growth.

Examples are provided to support you.

• Stage 1: Physiological needs

Example: Ensuring all pupils have access to nutritious meals through our breakfast club and subsidised lunch programme.

• Stage 2: Safety needs

Example: Implementing clear anti-bullying policies and procedures to ensure all pupils feel safe and respected.

• Stage 3: Social needs

Example: Hosting regular parent–teacher meetings and family events to strengthen school–home partnerships.

• Stage 4: Self-esteem

Example: Recognising and celebrating pupils' achievements through awards ceremonies and through our school newsletter/social media.

• Stage 5: Self-actualisation

Example: Supporting career guidance and work experience placements to help pupils pursue their aspirations.

📖 Further reading

Allen (2011) – 'Early intervention: The next steps'
Early Intervention Foundation (2023) – 'Why is it good for children and families?'
McLeod (2018) – 'Maslow's hierarchy of needs'

5 Displacement and poverty

Shayne Elsworth

Chapter summary

Schools have a pivotal role to play in ensuring that displaced young people find belonging and safety and are supported to be academically successful. Schools can be, and often are, a place of sanctuary for both pupils and their families. In this chapter we look at the needs and challenges of asylum seekers and refugees and how best to support them.

 What does the research suggest?

There is a growing body of research on how schools can support displaced young people. Below is a sample of research that we have found useful in our work with displaced pupils facing multiple poverty-related barriers to learning.

Research 1

Refugee Education UK (2023)

'Inclusive and Sustainable Promising Practices in Refugee Education (InSPPiRE): Learnings from case studies in high income settings'

Whilst a disproportionate number of refugees are hosted in low- and middle-income countries, the UK is home to some of the 22 per cent of refugees hosted in high-income settings. Based at the University of Nottingham, the Inclusive and Sustainable Promising Practices in Refugee Education (InSPPiRE) project, a partnership with Refugee Education UK, has identified promising practice and key learning from 29 case studies in 12 different countries. This is a helpful starting point for creating an inclusive and supportive culture and an excellent summary of best practice.

Key points

This research identifies four core themes:

- **Access to quality education in the national education system:** This first theme is of course about getting into educational provision as quickly as possible, but also about providing enhanced language support, assessing ability to ensure that provision is most appropriate and facilitating cultural orientation to ensure rapid assimilation.

- **Psychosocial wellbeing and inclusive practices:** This recognises the impact of trauma and hardship, promoting trauma-informed approaches, working with external specialists and ensuring there is a safe culture in which pupils are welcomed and have appropriate cultural representation.

- **Educator training and support:** This recognises the importance of teachers being equipped to play their part. Local and national partnerships add value here.

- **Partnerships for sustainable outcomes:** This recognises the need for a wide range of services to work together as the only effective way to tackle intersectional poverty. The final promising practice, establishing a school as a hub of community support, is one that truly enriches and benefits the whole setting.

Research 2

Gladwell and Chetwynd (2018)

'Education for refugee and asylum-seeking children: Access and equality in England, Scotland and Wales'

This report, reflecting the experiences of 86 children across all phases of education, gives readers an insight into the effectiveness of access and equality in UK schools.

The UK's statutory guidance recommends that all looked-after children, including unaccompanied asylum-seeking children, should be placed in education as soon as possible when entering care, to minimise the impact of missed education. But this is rarely achieved, with up to a quarter of children waiting over three months for a secondary school or college place. At an individual level, there are some barriers to access, which include SEND and (disappointingly) a reluctance to admit pupils into Key Stage 4 due to fear of adversely affecting performance tables. The development of a school-wide ethos to welcome refugees and asylum-seeking children has been shown to have a positive impact on admissions and on advocating for these children.

Key points

Recommendations from this report are predominantly aimed at central government, but there are still several helpful suggestions. These include:

- ensuring that all teachers receive training as standard to increase understanding
- ensuring that young people are connected to a supportive peer and wider youth networks
- ensuring that schools are aware that these pupils do not impact on their results profile (their results can be removed from performance tables).

Research 3

Ashlee et al. (2022)

'Finding their way: The journey to university for refugee and asylum-seeking young people in Coventry'
Only six per cent of refugees worldwide have access to higher education (HE), compared to the global average of 40 per cent. This research explores the potential of a localised approach to understanding and addressing the barriers to higher education experienced by refugees and asylum seekers.

Key points

The research indicates that many of these young people are ambitious and strive towards studying in further and higher education; however, these young people face considerable barriers. Two of the three most significant barriers to accessing HE for refugees and asylum seekers are no different to any other disadvantaged group: culture and cost.

- **Culture:** The research suggests that universities should work with schools and colleges to ensure that pupils feel that they belong on campus, that they count themselves in the university culture and feel welcomed into the institution. Simple outreach actions, such as welcoming refugee and asylum-seeking young people onto campuses, can help to shift perceptions of universities as unwelcoming to being settings that celebrate diversity. Accompanying these outreach experiences with a peer mentor could further empower these pupils. There is a significant opportunity here for partnerships between schools/colleges and their local universities.

- **Costs:** The research shines a light on practical ways to support pupils with the costs of HE, including the need for universities to rethink their fees, e.g. some universities charge all forced migrants home fees, rather than the international pupil rate.

The other significant barrier is that of language acquisition, with refugees and asylum seeker pupils disadvantaged by a lack of academic language. This has been shown to limit access to university and result in pupils being unable to engage in academic discussion about their subject. There is a challenge here to ensure that ESOL (English for Speakers of Other Languages) support does not stop when pupils become fluent in English, but rather further education should be supplemented by academic language support.

Other useful research

- **Gladwell et al. (2021):** Perhaps unsurprisingly, further research illustrates a strong link between pupil outcomes and their socioeconomic status. For displaced pupils in particular, the most significant factor is stability of status, with settled refugees achieving significantly more highly.

- **Lambrechts (2020):** Not having secured settled status is just one of a multitude of factors that could inhibit refugee and asylum seekers from achieving their full educational potential. In numerous studies, researchers acknowledge the complexity of this intersectional poverty and the fact that it is never one single inhibiting factor, but rather that young people are facing multiple inhibiting factors simultaneously: a condition Lambrechts terms 'super-disadvantaged'.

- **Prentice (2022):** For multifaceted disadvantage, it makes sense that there should be a multifaceted approach to tackling it. Prentice (2022) suggests that the schools who see the most success academically enlist a range of holistic practices which relate both to academic progress and to non-academic well being.

Research takeaways

- Pupils who experience displacement (e.g. refugees, asylum seekers) can miss a significant period of education, so enrolment, assessment and support to assimilate to a new culture need to be rapid in schools.
- Language acquisition is an obvious need in resettlement but should not stop when pupils are fluent. Academic success requires academic language at times.
- A holistic approach to pupils' wellbeing is necessary to understand specific barriers to academic achievement and support pupils to overcome these.
- Teachers require training and support to understand how to meet the needs of refugees and asylum seekers in the classroom.

 Case Study

Bede Academy – School of Sanctuary

Bede Academy is an all–through multi-academy trust in the North of England. In 2021, Bede Academy in Blyth joined a growing national network of schools and colleges to become a School of Sanctuary. In 2019, Bede Academy welcomed three Syrian refugees. In 2023, this increased to 40 displaced pupils from Syria, Afghanistan and Ukraine.

The academy works in close partnership with the resettlement officers from the asylum seeker and refugee team, and in particular with the Northumberland EAL (English as an additional language) team. Using the four themes suggested by Refugee Education UK (see Research 1, page 72) to frame our experience, this case study explores some of the promising practices in our collective endeavours.

Power of relationship

To ensure provision is inclusive, there are no assumptions made about the barriers pupils are facing. When difficulties arise, letters are not responded to or homework is not completed, the first step is always an exploratory conversation. It is the power of relationships with leaders trained specifically to support EAL students that has enabled the academy to identify a range of cultural barriers to overcome. Some of the barriers that these pupils face are obvious but, crucially, there are others which may be overlooked.

Culture of pupils

Routines around the academy are reviewed by thinking about the culture of all pupils to ensure equitable access and support. Practical examples include changes to routines so that pupils who are fasting do not have to go through the refectory, or ensuring food is halal so that there are no barriers to catering for any pupil.

Other identified barriers have included:

- uniform that has required modifications (particularly PE kits for greater modesty)
- the perception of music and other areas of the curriculum
- understanding the value of studying other languages
- integrating with pupils of the opposite sex
- staying away from the family home on residential experiences
- the cost of living and access to practical and financial help.

Professional development

Asking ourselves how we can serve pupils more successfully forces us to be reflective about the inclusivity and effectiveness of our own classroom practice. The Northumberland EAL team and the academy have worked together to provide training for classroom teachers in terms of both general awareness and practical teaching strategies. There is both whole-school professional development and time spent with individual teams, which has built relationships and a culture of collective endeavour.

Each new year (or new arrival) begins with an introduction to Bede families, usually during in-service training days. Here, leaders in the academy confidentially and candidly share background knowledge of individual pupils and their context to enable teachers to plan for and respond to specific barriers.

Partnership with Northumberland EAL

Partnership with the Northumberland EAL team has added capacity for a significant amount of translation work across multiple languages. EAL specialists supporting in classrooms share feedback and advice. The academy leadership team amplify best practice of EAL learners and refine approaches to intervention and support for them.

Some of the more effective practical teaching strategies have included:

- translation work in advance of lessons
- live narration in slideshows during lessons
- tablets for translation and for the pupil to view classroom resources at their own pace
- laptops for home use
- use of library and dictionaries
- one-to-one tuition.

Pupil voice

Pupils themselves have been pivotal in enabling the wider community to be aware of their experiences and the difficulties they have faced. Pupils have used assemblies to tell their stories and share experiences with their peers. Leaders in the academy have listened to the lived experiences of pupils and their families in the local community and designed lessons to combat incidents of prejudice and ignorance. Pupil voice and understanding of their lived experience is used to reframe and reshape the wider curriculum. For example, in religious studies, pupils explore war and conflict, Islamophobia and identity to address misconceptions that pupils and staff might have. A bespoke personal development programme tackles misconceptions head on, with responsive lessons dealing with issues such as racism and prejudice as they occur in the wider community.

Partnerships for sustainable outcomes

Design of provision at the academy is a collaborative endeavour and is strengthened by a wide range of partnerships with national charities, local providers and individuals with lived experience.

As alluded to throughout the case study, one of the most valuable partnerships has been that with the Northumberland EAL and resettlement teams. Their expertise, local knowledge, direct relationships with families and capacity to visit homes and attend meetings has been crucial in shaping and constantly reviewing provision.

Families are increasingly involved in the wider life of the academy. A recent cooking event, hosted in the food and nutrition classroom, saw around 12 families prepare traditional cuisine from around the globe, which became a banquet for invited families and staff. Parents really valued the opportunity to build relationships, share aspects of their own heritage and discuss ways of encouraging and supporting their children. The school–home relationship has continued to flourish, with even more families attending a subsequent coffee and cake event. It is worthwhile organising a series of social events to maintain this.

Long-term vision

There is a long-term vision to supporting pupils, from their arrival at the academy and initial displacement to flourishing in life beyond the academy. The EAL team call this 'playing the long game'. Five years after receiving the first displaced families, the academy is proud of the contribution these children and their families have made to the whole community. To date, the first six displaced pupils to leave Bede Academy have each secured places on university degree courses across the UK.

The first pupil with refugee experience to leave the academy was Haneen. She was inspirational in her approach to her studies. She attended both Year 10 and 11 classes to ensure she received as much teaching as possible, to enable her to succeed. This required a personalised timetable and careful consideration of the number of GCSE subjects she would study. During her A level studies, she also became a mentor to younger new arrivals and in between studies has worked as a teaching assistant in the academy. She began Year 11 with very little English, yet within a year achieved two grade 9s and four grade 8s. She left Bede Academy in 2021 and has gone on to study pharmacy at a local university. Her brother Anas has also had exceptional academic success. He left Bede Academy in 2022 to study civil engineering at Newcastle University. In addition to his studies, Anas has become a young leader with a local charity called Leading Link. The charity runs holiday provision for disadvantaged young people across Blyth in Northumberland.

Evlina joined Bede Academy in 2018, and left in summer 2023. As part of her studies, Evlina created this painting. It is a 3.6 m by 2.5 m mural sited in the academy's courtyard. The painting depicts a smiling girl, whom Evlina called *Ronahi*, which comes from the Kurdish word for light. *Ronahi* is painted alongside a lotus flower, which symbolises darkness, death and the absence of colour. There is further symbolism in white doves, which represent peace, fidelity and love, and a canary, which symbolises light and illumination to those who are lost. Evlina's message is that the smile of hope is stronger than our hardships. *Ronahi* looks to the light, and the smile that blooms in the dark can last a lifetime. Evlina currently studies architecture at Liverpool University.

Understanding individual needs

As the population of displaced pupils within our community grows, so too does the range of barriers and support needed to overcome the 'super-disadvantage' that they face. Some of these barriers are explored more extensively in Chapters 1 and 3. This case study from Bede Academy serves to share some of the effective practice developed in recent years, but should not be interpreted as a blueprint or held up as a paragon of best practice. We seek to understand the individual needs of our families, particularly those who face greater levels of disadvantage, and respond to them accordingly within our gift. It is hoped that by sharing this research and these strategies, you can reflect on what barriers your displaced pupils and their families might face and, crucially, consider what is in your gift to help overcome these. Our experience is that these pupils are some of the humblest, most appreciative and most rewarding to work with. They enrich our community, and we are privileged to walk a few years with them.

 Ideas to try

Welcome process

Suggestions

- Use assemblies and key dates (such as Refugee Week) to highlight the benefits of a welcoming and inclusive community and ethos.
- Set up a home visit if possible. Gather as much information as you can, including previous experiences of school, interests and literacy levels (in home language and English).
- Arrange a welcome meeting that the whole family attend. In the meeting, provide uniform, discuss curriculum, tour the site, alleviate specific worries and plan their induction.
- Consider a mid-week start. It gives pupils a shorter first week and helps them to navigate the new culture.
- Carefully select a peer who can meet the pupil on arrival and be their buddy throughout the day.

Language acquisition

Suggestions

- Seat new displaced pupils with a pupil who speaks articulately and clearly.
- Place pupils in classrooms with high levels of academic vocabulary and discussion, with individualised support, and only move into lower sets according to academic ability if necessary, once early stages of language acquisition are complete.

- Establish one-to-one tutoring, additional small-group support and bespoke homework tasks to help pupils progress at an accelerated rate.
- We have had pupils achieve top grades but be turned down from university because they were unable to discuss their subject in depth. Pupils studying A level might need to receive specific subject specialist support with academic language acquisition.
- Practise using subtitle features when displaying video or slideshow content. This is commonly available in most software.
- Identify a colleague or service who can speak fluently in the language of your pupils. Invite them to help with more nuanced translation of tier 3 vocabulary, key documents and assessments.

Homework interventions

Suggestions

- Provide homework support from a language specialist to overcome language barriers.
- Create early morning and after-school drop-in sessions for support with organisation of equipment and planning of homework.
- Provide access to IT facilities before and after school to overcome a lack of digital access at home.
- Use sixth form mentors or tutors to provide support for students who lack access to academic support at home.

Chapter takeaways

- Establish a welcoming ethos and regularly narrate the culture you hope for. Identify the benefits of a welcoming community where everyone is valued.
- Foster partnerships and build relationships proactively with families and other professionals connected with them, to build trust and mutual understanding of expectations and routines.

- Accelerate language acquisition by ensuring pupils are immersed in high-quality conversational language, with high levels of support and additional carefully sequenced intervention.

- Make no assumptions about potential barriers to engagement. Ask questions each time something is not returned, incomplete or unsuccessful, to understand the precise barrier.

- Create opportunities to serve. Pupils are aspirational and hopeful for their future; capture this infectious zest for life and help it to rub off on others.

Recap and Reflective tasks

Recap

Indicate which statements are true or false based on your understanding.	True	False
Intensive language support is essential and can be withdrawn once pupils are fluent in English.		
Refugee and asylum-seeking children are likely to aspire to higher education (university).		
Cultural barriers can prevent some pupils from fully engaging with the full breadth of the National Curriculum, particularly religious education, music and physical education.		
Displaced families are hard to reach and reluctant to engage with the school.		
Other professionals may be able to identify barriers to education more successfully than the school can.		

Reflective tasks

Reflective task for leaders and teacher educators
• What are the barriers faced by displaced pupils in your school? Do any of these pupils face more than one barrier simultaneously? Examples might include language barriers, poverty-related barriers to learning, discrimination or bullying.

Displacement and poverty

- Which pupils face super-disadvantage (where multiple disadvantages intersect)?

- Consider representation across your school community. Is the culture of pupils known, shared and understood? What opportunities could you create to enable every culture to be seen?

- How can you harness the engagement and enthusiasm of displaced pupils to support and empower others?

Practical application task

Consider each of the four themes identified by Refugee Education UK (see Research 1):

1. Access to quality education in the national education system
2. Psychosocial wellbeing and inclusive practices
3. Educator training and support
4. Partnerships for sustainable outcomes.

- Where do the strengths of your provision lie?

- What barriers persist in each of these areas?

- Who is best placed to further investigate these barriers and explore possible solutions?

- Which services work most closely with displaced families in your community?

- How could you strengthen relationships between school, families and other stakeholders?

Reflective task for teachers/curriculum leaders

- Which languages do your pupils speak and who can communicate with them when you cannot?

- How effective is support for pupils in the early stages of language acquisition?

- Has progression through tier 3 vocabulary been explicitly planned in the curriculum? How can you use this to create opportunities for ongoing language support?

- Are you/your colleagues proficient in the effective use of tools for translation, including live narration?

- What are the aspirations, hopes and dreams of the displaced pupils in your school? How can you support them towards these aspirations?

Practical application task
Reflect on your provision for the displaced pupils in your school and/or class.
- How much do you know about them?

- What do you need to know about them to be able to meet their needs effectively in the classroom?

- How effective is your provision for pupils who are fluent in another language, but not in English?

- Could you further reduce the language barrier by considering ways of using translation to enable pupils at the early stages of language acquisition to develop subject knowledge?

📖 Further reading

Gladwell (2021) – 'The impact of educational achievement on the integration and wellbeing of Afghan refugee youth in the UK'

McIntyre (2023) – 'Promoting the inclusion of refugee children in schools: Recommendations for secondary education policy in England'

Prentice (2022) – 'Educators' interactions with refugee pupils: Knowledge, attitudes, and practices'

Links

Bell Foundation – the Bell Foundation is a charity focused on reducing exclusion through language education. It collaborates with partners to develop policy, conduct research, provide training and implement practical interventions aimed at supporting individuals who speak English as an Additional Language: www.bell-foundation.org.uk

Hub for Education for Refugees in Europe: https://hubhere.org

Refugee Council: www.refugeecouncil.org.uk

School of Sanctuary: https://schools.cityofsanctuary.org

PART 2

Understanding and tackling poverty in the classroom

6 Poverty on the brain

Sara Davidson, Sean Harris

Chapter summary

Poverty is not just a social issue; it can impact all aspects of a child's life. In this chapter, we look at how poverty can impact the learning brain and what we can do in the classroom to help. We want to emphasise that this chapter does not endorse the notion that pupils can be educated out of poverty in classrooms. Understanding and addressing poverty within the context of schools requires a nuanced and complex approach, as explored in this book. However, as discussed in Chapter 2, the critical role of effective teaching and learning in classrooms cannot be overstated as part of a comprehensive strategy to overcoming the barriers to learning posed by poverty.

 What does the research suggest?

It is important to highlight that understanding and applying this research comes with caveats. Research shows that we should not assume that poverty impacts all children and families in the same way (Montacute and Cullinane, 2021; Rowland, 2021; Wagmiller, 2015). Any action from this chapter must therefore be carefully implemented. We recommend that you use this chapter as a starting point and read into the research further. We also encourage you to develop understanding in consultation with SEND and multi-agency professionals.

Research 1

Hanson et al. (2015)

'Behavioural problems after early life stress: Contributions of the hippocampus and amygdala'

This research by Hanson et al. investigates the impact of early life stress (ELS) on the development of brain regions involved in socioemotional functioning, specifically the amygdala and hippocampus. The study explores how different forms of ELS (such as physical abuse, neglect or low socioeconomic status) affect these brain regions and subsequent behavioural outcomes in children.

The research was conducted at the University of Wisconsin-Madison. Over 100 children participated in the study across different risk groups and comparison groups. The study also included additional participants specifically recruited for understanding the effects of environmental change and emotional caregiving.

Hanson et al. looked at two parts of the brain (the amygdala and hippocampus) across a sample of children who had suffered different ELS. Hanson et al. were particularly interested in the ways in which physical abuse, early neglect and low socioeconomic status might affect brain development. They measured cumulative stress of children and their families via interviews. These results were then compared with children who had not suffered any of the forms of ELS we mentioned earlier.

Key points

- Smaller amygdala volumes were found for children who had experienced ELS.

- Smaller hippocampus volumes were present for some children who had experienced physical abuse or were from households with low socioeconomic status.

- Along with another study by Hanson et al. (2013), the findings suggest that living in sustained poverty can place some children at high risk of problems across a variety of domains, including schooling, self-regulation and health.

Research 2

Blair and Raver (2016)

'Poverty, stress and brain development: New directions for prevention and intervention'

Blair and Raver and their team conducted a comprehensive review of how poverty affects children's thinking skills, brain development and early learning abilities. They conducted the research at the Department of Applied Psychology, New York University.

Key points

- One study in the review looked at 389 people aged between four and 22 years. They found that children in families in poverty had reduced grey matter volumes in the frontal and temporal cortex and the hippocampus area of the brain.

- Less grey matter in these areas of our brains can impact processing because it weakens memory functions and processing for everyday tasks.

- The reduction in grey matter applied to frontal and temporal lobes, which may have impacted some children's ability to solve problems, make decisions and even manage anger or impulse controls.

- The research also suggests that the effects of poverty on brain development may start early and can be seen in early childhood.

Research 3

Pensiero et al. (2021)

'Learning inequalities during the Covid-19 pandemic: A longitudinal analysis using the UK Understanding Society 2020 and 2021 data'

This study gives further evidence of how learning can be impacted by poverty. Whilst not directly linked to cognitive science or the brain, this research provides a relevant example of how learning can be significantly impacted by socioeconomic status.

In 2020, society witnessed widespread disruption to schools across the country as a result of the COVID-19 pandemic. Schools worked hard to maintain provision for all pupils, but many were forced to move to hybrid ways of learning with limited notice. Research indicates that the transition to these modes of learning affected millions of children across the country and many families struggled with the demands of home learning and society-wide disruption.

Pensiero et al. researched the ways in which lockdown impacted learning, particularly for children in low-income families.

Key points

- School disruption and home learning exacerbated inequalities by socioeconomic status.

- The impact of disadvantage was amplified when considering children's access to computers, family circumstances and parental working patterns.

Other useful research

- **Schmidt et al. (2021) Society to Cell:** This research highlights the global impact of child poverty, exacerbated by events like the COVID-19 pandemic. Poverty not only results in immediate health and developmental challenges but also increases the long-term risk of chronic diseases and mental health issues across the lifespan. The study reviews how poverty can biologically embed itself early in life, influencing physiological systems such as brain development and immune function.

- **Nobel et al. (2015): Family income, parental education and brain structure in children and adolescents:** This research involved over 1,000 individuals aged three to 20 years. Researchers found that income levels could be linked to brain surface area: smaller income differences had a more pronounced impact on surface area amongst children from lower-income families compared to those from higher-income backgrounds. These effects were particularly notable in brain regions crucial for language, reading, executive functions and spatial skills. The study suggests that income disparities correlate with brain structure, especially amongst socioeconomically disadvantaged children, and that these structural differences may contribute to varying neurocognitive abilities.

- **Perkins et al. (2024): Language processing following childhood poverty:** This study investigated how childhood poverty affects language abilities and brain function in adulthood. The research involved over 50 adults from a longitudinal study that began when they were nine years old. Through behavioural phonological awareness tasks and brain imaging during language processing, the study found that adults who grew up in poverty exhibited lower language skills and different patterns of brain activation compared to those from middle-income backgrounds. These findings indicate that the impacts of childhood poverty on the brain's language processing systems persist into adulthood.

Research takeaways

- Poverty is not just a social issue. It can impact learning, memory and processing.
- This impact comes from an accumulation of factors and the length of exposure to different facets of poverty.

- The research explored in this chapter does not state that every child in poverty will be impacted in these ways. School leaders and teachers need to carefully interpret this research. It needs to be considered alongside an understanding of pupil need as explored in other chapters. A forensic understanding of the needs of children must sit alongside interpretation of this chapter in schools.

 ## Case Study

Dormanstown Primary Academy and Wilton Primary Academy

A professional development programme was created to help teachers and support staff understand how poverty and disadvantage can affect children's learning. The programme included sharing local poverty statistics and asking staff to identify what they already knew or didn't know about poverty in the local community. Teachers and support staff were given time to explore research on this topic. This included access to the research, articles and thinking explored in the research section of this chapter.

Following this, the programme focused on developing effective teaching practices. Staff learned about the principles of the science of learning and how it impacts lesson planning and teaching. The training highlighted several crucial teaching habits, such as breaking down learning goals, building on prior knowledge and making learning stick in long-term memory through retrieval routines. Teachers practised these skills together using the concept of a pre-mortem, where they considered questions such as:

- What are the main ideas or concepts of the lesson that I want pupils to understand?
- What might all pupils struggle with?
- What might pupils struggle with because of their experience of hardship or poverty?
- How can I support pupils to embed this learning in their long-term memory?
- Which worked examples can we use in our classrooms to help pupils understand the learning goal or desired outcome?

Teachers and leaders applied these habits in their lesson and curriculum planning, using research-based tools and strategies such as unit assessments, pre-tests, pre-mortems, scaffolding and spaced retrieval. By focusing on these habits, they aimed to make learning more accessible, especially for disadvantaged pupils, and to improve pupils' problem-solving and decision-making skills. The training provided teachers and support staff with an opportunity to understand research into poverty and the learning brain. It also allowed teachers and support staff to consider this in relation to their own classroom environments and make use of other data sources to understand the actual needs of pupils, as opposed to making assumptions that all pupils would face the same barriers. It presented staff with an opportunity to then explore, understand and practise actual habits in classrooms that would support pupils struggling with aspects of learning, memory or processing.

 Ideas to try

Schools are in the business of learning. It follows then that teachers and leaders in schools are well-placed to be able to respond to some of the research summarised in this chapter. However, we do want to stress that schools cannot simply teach pupils out of poverty. Poverty is more nuanced and complex than this, as explored throughout other parts of this book.

It is important for teaching and learning to be a central part of tackling poverty in schools and this is explored further in Chapter 2. Given the complexities of neurology and the caveats explored in this chapter, it would be misleading to suggest that there is a one-size-fits-all approach for every classroom or cohort of pupils. However, there are a range of strategies for facilitating effective learning which may support pupils impacted by poverty. These are not 'silver bullets' but they do provide an actionable approach for teachers and leaders wanting to tackle some of the poverty-related barriers to learning.

Diagnose pupil needs in the classroom

It is important to ensure that teachers and leaders have identified the barriers to learning that children are facing. Teachers need to understand these barriers and how they impact a pupil in the classroom. This is explored more fully in Chapter 1.

Suggestions

- Make sure that the needs and barriers to learning are determined from assessment and not merely based on guesswork or assumptions.
- Speak to the SENDCo and other professionals who have a holistic view of individual pupils, as applicable. (See Chapter 4 for more on this.)

Make retrieval routine in learning

Research indicates that retrieval practice can help to facilitate effective learning (Roediger and Karpicke, 2006). If poverty does impact memory and processing, then it is important to support pupils' recall and use of previously taught learning. Retrieval practice is one example of how teachers can support learning brains to both recall and retain information.

Here are some examples:

Low-stakes quizzing

- Create simple and short low-stakes quizzes in lessons to support recall and retrieval.
- Ensure the quizzes are accessible to all pupils, especially those who may face additional barriers to learning.
- Try planning a stock of low-stakes quiz questions as a subject or phase team.
- Remind pupils (and teachers) that these quizzes are designed to support retrieval in a low-stakes environment. Encourage pupils to attempt the tasks rather than only affirming the top points earners or those who complete the activity quickly.

Self-explanation

- Ask pupils to explain a recently taught concept. Give pupils independent practice time to prepare for this. This might include something simple such as: 'Outline what we learned yesterday about the Roman Empire.'
- Alternatively, you could task pupils with something that requires more thought and articulation, e.g. 'Prepare a 60-second summary of what you learned about effective strategies for making cities sustainable.'

- The important aspect of these challenges is to provide pupils with an opportunity to generate a version of what they understand from a previous aspect of taught material and learning. The process of mental rehearsal and re-articulation is important as it challenges pupils to use their cognitive abilities to consolidate previous learning before accessing new learning.

- These tasks can also be structured as homework tasks to support retrieval outside of lessons.

Dilute auditory distractions in the classroom

Focus in classrooms is crucial. Simons and Chabris (1999) demonstrated that focusing on a single task can cause people to miss other important details. A pupil dealing with the challenges of poverty might have trouble focusing and concentrating. To help pupils, especially those who struggle with attention and processing, we should guide them to concentrate on tasks. Here are some suggestions that might help.

Suggestions

- Classrooms do not need to always be silent; peer interaction is really important. However, try to create distinct opportunities for collaborative learning and for pupils to complete tasks independently and without distraction.

- Before asking pupils to discuss a question or topic with a peer, ensure that they have at least a minute or two to consider their own response to the question. This can support more meaningful talk between pupils but can also help pupils to focus on the question being asked. It can further limit pupils feeling under pressure by being put on the spot or expected to give an answer that has not been thought through. This pressure can cause an additional distraction for some pupils in classrooms.

- Research from Wood et al. (2012) shows that attempting to engage pupils in two non-related tasks at once can hinder learning. In our experience working in schools, we have seen teachers talk over pupils during quiet independent practice or ask pupils to read from presentation slides whilst giving them multiple instructions. This is easily done as a teacher and we have done this ourselves, but it can be distracting and confusing. Instead, ask pupils to read the content on the presentation first before talking about it, or set specific time in the lesson to read the content.

- Pupils might say that radio and music 'helps us learn' or 'helps us stay on task'. Research indicates that it is unlikely to support learning and it can even inhibit the conditions for learning (Perham and Currie, 2014). Next time a pupil suggests this, make a point of sharing that research actually debunks the myth that listening to music whilst engaged in studies will help learning. Music, unless central to the learning task, is by definition background noise and splits the attention of the brain.

Dilute visual distractions

It is not just talk or sound that can be distracting; think about visual distractions as well.

Suggestions

- **Avoid crowded displays:** As creative beings, too often we want to fill an empty canvas or wall space with learning posters or displays of pupil work. This is well-intentioned, but consider how much it actually adds value to the learning and to pupils' focus. Crowded displays can add to your workload and, most likely, to the cognitive load of your pupils.
- **Keep classroom focus points uncluttered:** Consider the display of work around a whiteboard or central focus point in the classroom (e.g. teacher board). If you want to direct pupils' attention purposefully, then try to avoid work or school notices surrounding these visual areas. (We once visited a school that took pride in the motivational messages that pupils and colleagues were given as part of their commitment to the culture and ethos of the school. Almost every screen or whiteboard in the school had several motivational metaphors and quotes surrounding the board. It may have helped some pupils and teachers feel motivated but, according to feedback from the pupils themselves, 'It makes concentrating in lessons really hard because you try and remember the quotes and who might have said them instead!').
- **Avoid animated objects and text in presentations:** In an attempt to make presentation slides or screen-based tasks more creative and appealing, many of us will fall into the trap of adding an animated image (or additional noise). These are likely contributing to the additional strain on brains for pupils needing to focus and concentrate. Incidentally, this applies to staff meetings too. If we want to model the type of learning environment that supports strained brains, then it is important we demonstrate this in staff training sessions.

- **Keep things simple where possible:** Provide a brief summary of key points. This supports learning more effectively than large amounts of text and avoids too much cognitive overload.

Avoid overload

Pupils' brains have a capacity limit. If you are not convinced, let a bee into a classroom and watch the impact on the attention span of both teacher and pupils! Too often, we can fall into the trap of thinking that more exposure to new knowledge is the only way to ensure that brains are ready for learning.

One school that we supported insisted on subject knowledge top-up sessions for almost two hours before each GCSE exam across all exam subjects. Teachers would cover vast amounts of GSCE specifications in hundreds of presentation slides in an attempt to ensure that all pupils were primed to answer any given question set in the exam.

Whilst the strategy was well-intentioned, it added to cognitive strain and stress for some pupils, particularly those facing poverty-related barriers to learning. Furthermore, there was no correlation to show that it improved pupils' achievement and it arguably led some pupils to be cognitively overloaded ahead of an exam.

Instead, consider how taught content can be connected to previously learned topics and ideas. This is discussed further in the following information about consolidating concepts.

Try 'SUM', a three-stage process that can support pupils in reading and summarising information from teacher resources (e.g. a presentation or book). This can be useful if pupils are being presented with a lot of information, text or ideas.

S	Pupils **skim-read** the information at least twice independently before the teacher introduces tasks/ activities linked to the information.	Teacher instruction: Explain to pupils that this involves reading quickly to get a brief understanding of the text/information.

U	Pupils **use** their own words to summarise the main points into two to five bullet points.	Teacher instruction: Explain to pupils that this should not involve simply copying the information. Ask pupils to use bullet points or similar methods.
M	Pupils note the **main** ideas only.	Teacher instruction: Explain to pupils that you will ask them to verbally summarise the main points from their summary.

Suggestions

- Evidence suggests that pupils need to encounter concepts and complex content multiple times before they can begin to learn it (Karpicke, 2009). As curriculum, phase and subject leaders, identify the key concepts that will support learning future content. Concepts should not simply be a vast list of subject vocabulary. For example, in maths, you might identify long-multiplication and division as core, complex concepts.

- Once concepts are mapped for a topic or unit, work out where these concepts can be revisited and further connected. This is especially important for pupils who may have limited exposure to these concepts or extra-curricular experiences due to poverty or low income. For example, teachers serving in coastal community areas with high levels of poverty might over-expose pupils to barriers facing coastal towns because they are aware that not many families have access to the beach.

- Build regular opportunities through lesson planning and delivery for pupils to make deliberate links between concepts in multiple schemes of work. This is important for helping pupils to connect big ideas and complex concepts. For example, an exploration of the Holocaust in history may draw on the concepts of social justice and equality. These are concepts that can be consolidated through subjects such as RE, English or PSHE. A unit in science about the human digestive system might be taught through the concepts of health, systems and process. Consider how these concepts could be further developed in other units and through subjects such as PE, computer science or sport science.

Chapter takeaways

- There are no 'silver bullets' to addressing poverty in classrooms, but there are principles for effective learning that can be used to support learning.
- Ensure that teachers and support staff accurately identify and understand the specific barriers to learning faced by each pupil. Base this on what is known about individual pupils' needs rather than assumptions.
- Through thoughtful planning and curriculum design, focus on deconstructing learning objectives, building upon existing knowledge and incorporating retrieval practices to reinforce and solidify learning in long-term memory.
- Avoid overcrowded displays in the classroom, as they can increase both teacher workload and pupil cognitive load, potentially hindering focus and learning.
- Keep central focus points like whiteboards/screens uncluttered to ensure pupils' attention is directed effectively without distraction.
- Simplify presentations and avoid unnecessary animations or background music, to reduce cognitive strain and support learning effectiveness.

Recap and Reflective tasks

Recap

Indicate which statements are true or false based on your understanding.	True	False
Research demonstrates that all children living in poverty will have less capacity to learn new knowledge and information.		
Influences of poverty on brain development come from an accumulation of factors and the length of exposure to these social environments.		
Retrieval practice must always take the form of a quiz at the start of a new lesson or at the end of a lesson.		
Creating deliberate opportunities for background noise (e.g. music) will almost always support learning and pupils using independent practice time in lessons.		

Reflective tasks

Reflective task for leaders and teacher educators
• To what extent is retrieval practice understood and built into learning in classrooms? • To what extent is a science of learning understood by new and established teachers in the school – especially in relation to managing distractions and conceptual development?

Learning/classroom visit
Identify a core group of pupils who leaders/teachers recognise are impacted by aspects of poverty and/or disadvantage. This must be managed sensitively and carefully. Invite leaders, a SENDCo and curriculum leaders to trail the learning diet that these pupils get across the breadth of the school day. In this example, this refers to visiting lessons as part of a diet walk. More detail on diet walks can be found on page 20.

- Where were the deliberate opportunities for retrieval practice to support learning?

- What concepts were pupils exposed to and how were these carefully identified, communicated or connected as part of learning in subject areas?

- To what extent was additional turbulence, disruption or distraction managed?

- How did this appear to support learning?

Reflective task for teachers/curriculum leaders

- What are your main takeaways from this chapter in relation to your own subject area(s)?

- Think about a key unit/topic for a specific year group.
- Identify which concepts pupils will be introduced to as part of this unit

Topic/unit of study	Key concepts that pupils will encounter
E.g. Who were the Romans?	Empire: Pupils exploring the empire as political structures, often encompassing multiple territories and diverse populations, governed by a single supreme authority, usually an emperor or empress, exercising centralised control. Invasion: Pupils exploring invasion as aggressive entrance of armed forces into a territory with the intent to conquer, occupy or assert control over it. Infrastructure: Pupils exploring infrastructure as the essential systems and structures, such as roads, bridges and water supply, that support the functioning and development of a society or nation.

Topic/unit of study	Key concepts that pupils will encounter

- Next, consider where concepts might be revisited in further areas of study and/or in other curriculum areas.

Concept	Other topics/content	Other subject areas
Poverty Equality Injustice	*Oliver Twist* *A Christmas Carol* *An Inspector Calls*	RE: Poverty and equality PSHE: Caring for others Charity week in school Geography: Global poverty

Dealing with distractions: • Carry out a visit to your classroom or the classrooms shared by your team. Identify any additional distractions or noisy environments that might be better managed.	
Potential distraction	How can we manage the distractions better?
Example: • Lots of posters and key words written around the display board	Examples: • Put key words at the back of the room. • Add key words to a slide/display only displayed when we want pupils to draw on these words. • Have a key vocabulary sheet in pupils' books only.

📖 Further reading

Hackman and Farah (2009) – 'Socioeconomic status and the developing brain'

Hanson et al. (2013) – 'Family poverty affects the rate of human infant brain growth'

Harris (2022) – 'Poverty on the brain: Five strategies to counter the impact of disadvantage'

7 Crafting curriculum
Darren Higgins, Stuart Mayle

Chapter summary

A significant amount of work has taken place in recent years around curriculum development and design. Curriculum can be a key lever for tackling poverty and disadvantage in schools. In this chapter, we explore some of the specific research and principles to using curriculum to help tackle poverty-related barriers to learning.

 What does the research suggest?

Research summarised in this chapter indicates that some poverty-related barriers to learning can be tackled through a rigorous curriculum. Schools need to provide high-quality and academic curricula that are taught effectively (see the previous chapter). Pupils also need opportunities and experiences in school that poverty and disadvantage may otherwise have prevented them from accessing.

Research 1

Counsell (2018)

'Taking curriculum seriously'

Christine Counsell is a prominent figure in education and has contributed significantly to curriculum development and history education.

In an article named 'Taking curriculum seriously', published with the Chartered College of Teaching, Counsell talks about her experience of building a trust-wide knowledge-rich curriculum. Her insights remind curriculum leaders that understanding and mapping the knowledge you want pupils to learn is vital. The distinction between substantive and disciplinary knowledge can help curriculum leaders and teachers with this.

Key points

- Substantive knowledge can be treated as established fact.

- Disciplinary knowledge is what pupils learn about how that knowledge was established, its degree of certainty and how it continues to be revised by scholars, artists or professional practice.

- Disciplinary knowledge helps pupils understand that substantive knowledge is subject to change. This can support pupils in being critical of the curriculum choices made and lead to a shared understanding that the truth that they have been taught is not absolute.

- Curriculum can be associated with power. Decisions about what knowledge to teach are an exercise of power and an ethical responsibility. Curriculum leaders and teachers have an important but complex role in deciding what to teach.

Research 2

Erickson et al. (2017)

Concept-Based Curriculum and Instruction for the Thinking Classroom
Using examples from the classroom and research into learning, Erickson et al. write about the need for curriculum leaders to organise learning in a concepts-based curriculum.

Developing and delivering a concepts-based curriculum can be difficult and requires curriculum leaders and teachers to work collaboratively. This research provides a useful starting point for understanding why concepts are important and provides practical approaches to organising a curriculum in this way. Amongst other benefits, concepts allow pupils to make greater sense of content by making explicit links with pre-existing knowledge.

Erickson et al. provide practical steps for designing a concept-based curriculum unit, with extended explanations and examples to support teachers. There are a number of steps to this process, and we recommend that readers make use of their work in full to understand and be able to apply this effectively.

Key points

- **Ensure there is a specific unit title and focus:** This is helpful for focusing the topic and ensuring that disadvantaged pupils understand the context of the learning.

- **Identify the conceptual lens:** Using a conceptual framework can enhance the depth and focus of curriculum study. For example, in a history curriculum, identifying the conceptual lens of 'power dynamics' might support pupils with a focused and deeper exploration of historical events.

- **Break it down:** Identify interdisciplinary unit strands that will be included in each area of the curriculum. It is important that these are broken down into manageable parts so that they are understood by all teachers, leaders and pupils.

- **Map topics and concepts:** Think about units as a whole and map out the core concepts that underpin each topic. This then leads into teachers considering the facts, skills and resources needed.

Research 3

Organisation for Economic Co-operation and Development (2021a)

'Embedding values and attitudes in curriculum: Shaping a better future'

This report by the OECD presents data on curriculum, summarising existing literature and trends in curriculum change with challenges and strategies, and suggesting lessons learned from countries experienced with curriculum reforms. Understanding and embedding values (e.g. empathy, resilience and inclusivity) into the curriculum can support teachers in fostering supportive learning environments that promote positive outcomes for all pupils, especially those facing poverty-related barriers to learning. This approach not only enhances educational equity but also contributes to the development of skills and attitudes that are important for navigating challenges and barriers to learning.

Key points

- Clearly articulated and experienced values and attitudes can support pupils' positive lifelong learning outcomes and promote a more equitable society.

- Encourage pupils to develop critical thinking by exploring the contradictions or tensions inherent in subjects from various perspectives.
- Promote teamwork and cooperation through collaborative projects and challenges, such as group presentations.
- Develop responsibility by empowering pupils to make informed decisions about their own lives and their impact on others, for instance addressing local issues affecting the school community or their neighbourhood.
- Foster empathy by guiding pupils to share their thoughts, understand others' views and respond compassionately to others during lessons or constructive debate.
- Support resilience by helping individual pupils set goals that provide purpose and satisfaction in mastering tasks or new skills. The use of goal-setting in mentoring is explored in Chapter 12.

Other useful research

- **Turner (2016) Secondary Curriculum and Assessment Design:** Turner explores why curriculum is never complete. Research challenges the idea that curriculum can be marked as complete. It should be regularly reviewed and refined by leaders and teachers.
- **Wiliam (2013) Principled curriculum design:** Wiliam suggests that focusing on specific elements of subject matter allows for deeper understanding. This supports the long-term retention and application of knowledge in various contexts.
- **Hirsch (1999) The Schools We Need: And Why We Don't Have Them:** Hirsch suggests that a coherent and well-structured curriculum is important for achieving equity in classrooms. It can provide background knowledge for all pupils to achieve and participate fully in society.
- **McPhail and Rata (2015) Comparing curriculum types:** McPhail and Rata explore how pupils learn more effectively when it builds on what they already understand, and note that this is especially important to remember when considering the science of learning and crafting curriculum that looks to tackle poverty-related barriers to learning.

Research takeaways

- As teachers and school leaders, we are curriculum designers and developers. The distinction between substantive and disciplinary knowledge can help in the design and delivery of curriculum. For example, it might support teachers in mitigating the variability in curriculum or educational experiences that can arise from poverty-related barriers to learning.

- Concepts in curriculum can allow for pupils to make greater sense of content, make explicit links with pre-existing knowledge and be supported in applying this knowledge.

- A values-based curriculum warrants the attention of curriculum leaders, as it guides teachers in integrating important values or virtues alongside academic knowledge, nurturing well-rounded development in pupils regardless of their background or ability.

- Pupils learn more effectively when it builds on what they already understand. This is especially important to consider when comparing to the science of learning and crafting curriculum with poverty in mind.

 Case Study

Brambles Primary Academy – designing a history curriculum with poverty in mind

Brambles Primary Academy, located in Middlesbrough in the North of England, faces challenges due to rising child poverty and the high cost of living in the community. It is crucial for teachers to play an active role in designing and delivering a curriculum that supports children encountering poverty-related barriers to learning.

At our school, we challenge the notion that children and families lack ambition because of hardship or poverty in our communities. However, we recognise that many pupils lack the same opportunities and experiences as their peers from more affluent backgrounds. Therefore, our teachers have carefully considered this context when designing subjects like history. The curriculum is tailored to reflect our local community whilst striving to ensure that every pupil has equal access to knowledge, experiences and educational opportunities. Our curriculum also considers the importance of values to help support character development and virtues.

When we designed a curriculum around the theme of World War Two, we first of all wanted to think about key values and virtues children might gain. We chose a key question that supported empathy: How did children show resilience during World War Two?

We then identified the substantive knowledge that children and young people would need in order to answer that key question, both prior knowledge and new knowledge. This was important because it ensured that teachers could effectively plan and deliver lessons that equipped pupils with the foundational understanding needed to engage with the topics. For this topic, the substantive knowledge included 'fingertip knowledge' such as when World War Two started and ended. This built on prior knowledge about the chronology of Middlesbrough's industrial revolution and the Tudors. Additionally, the Tudors' impact on life in Britain was built on by substantive knowledge of how World War Two impacted lives in Britain.

Once we were happy that substantive knowledge was sufficiently layered and that it built on learning over time, we considered the disciplinary knowledge that would be taught throughout the topic. In history, this is how pupils can be historians. How do they enquire and engage with sources of evidence in order to build a schema around the key question and place the substantive knowledge within a broad context of history?

Disciplinary knowledge for the key question includes 'show an awareness of propaganda' as an example of historical interpretation and 'locate and analyse relevant information to justify claims about the past' as an example of sources of evidence. These skills allow pupils to interrogate the knowledge and question the authenticity as well as empathising with multiple sources of truth, in this case Allied versus Axis propaganda.

We wanted to support pupils in developing and retaining knowledge, reducing cognitive load and freeing the working memory. One way to do this was to ensure that we taught the key concepts in a range of topics and areas (Erickson et al., 2017 and Chapter 6 of this book). We checked that the World War Two topic linked to key concepts of 'Invasion and Empire' and 'Settlements and Social History', linked to substantive knowledge on world leaders and key leaders within a number of 'empires' and built on prior conceptual links such as Ancient Greece, Ancient Egypt and Vikings.

 Ideas to try

Curriculum in context

Consider the specific context of the community that a school serves. A one-size-fits-all approach to curriculum will not respond to the nuances of individual communities.

Suggestions

- **Understand the scale of disadvantage in the area:** We use a range of data publicly available to help understand some of the impacts of deprivation locally to our school. You could look at the English indices of deprivation and data available through organisations such as the Joseph Rowntree Foundation.

- **Consider employment rates and key employment areas in the community:** There may be local industries and enterprise projects that exist close to your school. Incorporate these considerations into your curriculum design to provide pupils with practical exposure to real-world applications linked to local businesses and industries. Practical examples of this are provided in Chapter 13.

Backwards design

Once a curriculum rationale is established, consider the context and goals outlined and explore what the intended outcomes are. What abilities or skills will be cultivated in the children and young people you serve?

Whilst the framework of curriculum is often heavily led by the National Curriculum, this merely outlines the 'matters, skills and processes' to be taught at each stage. Curriculum leaders can map out the substantive and disciplinary knowledge that are the stepping stones to understanding the overarching 'theme', e.g. 'The Roman Empire and its Impact on Britain' or 'The Development of Church, State and Society in Medieval Britain 1066–1509'. This structured approach can help to ensure that all pupils, including those facing poverty-related barriers to learning, have equitable access to a comprehensive curriculum that builds knowledge and skills.

Suggestions

- Use key questions to identify the end goal of a unit. What do you want pupils to be able to do or know at the end of the teaching sequence?

- Identify what pupils must know and be able to do in order to answer that question to help them learn effectively. What knowledge and skills do they need to have in order to reach that end point? (Substantive knowledge.) What are the key subject-specific skills and attributes that need to be developed in order to access or apply that substantive knowledge? (Disciplinary knowledge.)

- Support pupils in learning and retaining knowledge by creating links between topics and ensuring that new topics build on existing knowledge.

Tackling barriers to experiencing knowledge

Not all pupils can access a curriculum equitably. Picture an Early Years or Key Stage 1 pupil learning about the beach, discussing the feel of the sand, the way that the waves roll up the beach and lap at their toes, how the horizon curves away in the distance, how sand compacted in a bucket and turned over can be transformed into a castle. In some cases, misconceptions can remain unless knowledge is experienced. It may not be possible for pupils in all areas of the world and for all subjects to experience everything. However, it can be useful to ask questions like those below.

Suggestions

Try asking the following questions:

- What are the key experiences and encounters we need pupils to have in order to have equitable access to curriculum and life chances in later life?

- What are the key experiences your children miss out on due to geographic or financial disadvantage?

- What are the quick wins for experiences and encounters locally?

- Which are the key learning points your children need to truly experience to develop a clear and misconception-free schema? How is this manageable and mapped in your curriculum?

Chapter takeaways

- Curriculum must be responsive to the community context of the school. A one-size-fits-all approach is unlikely to be equitable or respond to specific poverty-related barriers to learning that pupils in your school face.
- Plan with the end in mind. Identify where pupils will need to be before thinking about what they need to know to get there.
- Build on prior knowledge to allow the development of schemas and reduce the cognitive load on pupils.
- Pupils require experiences and encounters and these can be used to close the gap between disadvantaged and less disadvantaged pupils.

Recap and Reflective tasks

Recap

Indicate which statements are true or false based on your understanding.	True	False
Breaking down curriculum content into granular and bite-sized detail will assist all pupils, particularly disadvantaged learners.		
Concepts in curriculum can allow for pupils to make greater sense of content, make explicit links with pre-existing knowledge and be supported in applying this knowledge.		
A one-size-fits-all-schools approach to curriculum should be encouraged, as it will have been most likely tested in other settings, therefore allowing for curriculum leaders to readily apply it to their own setting.		
Pupils learn more effectively when it builds on what they already understand. This is especially important when designing and developing curriculum.		

Reflective tasks

Reflective task for curriculum leaders and teachers
Identify one year group/phase in your school and a subject that pupils study. Next, consider a specific topic in the curriculum. Consider the key knowledge that forms part of this topic. An example is provided on the next page.

Example:	Example:
Year group: Year 7	Key knowledge:
Subject: Geography	Naming and recognising:
Topic: Map skills	• continents
	• oceans
	• countries
	• longitude
	• latitude

Now refer back to substantive and disciplinary knowledge and map the knowledge needed for this topic.

Substantive knowledge	Disciplinary knowledge
Example:	Example:
• To name and recognise continents, oceans and countries.	• To use grid references and a compass.
	• To use map symbols.
• To define longitude and latitude in relation to a map.	• To measure distance using map scale.

Next, consider the key concepts that you want pupils to understand in relation to this topic and where these are encountered in other areas of the curriculum/subject.

Concepts pupils will encounter:	Other areas of the subject/curriculum where pupils have been/will be exposed to these:

Finally, consider some of the possible barriers to understanding these concepts/topics and how you might support pupils to overcome these. Examples are provided.	
Possible barriers to learning the concept:	Ways in which teachers can help to tackle this:
Example: Concept: Location and place Potential barriers: Disadvantaged pupils might: • have limited travel experience beyond their local community • have limited use of electronic devices, so be unfamiliar with location or navigation software.	Example: • Adequate time given to demonstration and practice of map/navigation software in classroom or on computers. • Ensure that homework does not rely on pupils having access to software or adequate technology at home. • Build additional time into curriculum for reintroducing pupils to map symbols and use of maps, rather than assuming that they have secure knowledge of this.

📖 Further reading

Arthur et al. (2022) – 'Teaching character education: What works?'

Erickson (2002) – *Concept-Based Curriculum and Instruction: Teaching Beyond the Facts*

Harlen (2010) – 'Principles and big ideas for science education'

Harris (2021) – '*Crafting your curriculum with poverty in mind*'

Kennedy, J. (1995) – 'Debiasing the curse of knowledge in audit judgment'

Rata, E. (2015) – 'A pedagogy of conceptual progression and the case for academic knowledge'

Rich et al. (2017) – 'Belief in corrective feedback for common misconceptions: Implications for knowledge revision'

Wheelahan (2010) – *Why Knowledge Matters in the Curriculum*
Willingham (2009) – *Why Don't Pupils Like School?*
Young and Muller (2016) – *Curriculum and the Specialisation of Knowledge*

Links

Brambles Primary Academy: https://brambles.teesvalleyeducation.co.uk

Chartered College of Teaching, Rethinking Curriculum project – the Rethinking Curriculum project is a long-term initiative aimed at enhancing knowledge and skills within English primary education. It seeks to support teachers and school leaders by providing them with the tools to identify, plan and implement effective curriculum development tailored to their specific contexts. The goal is to offer all pupils a broad, engaging curriculum that fosters connections with local communities and supports their overall wellbeing and fulfilment: https://chartered.college/rethinkingcurriculum

8 Social justice and school culture

Louisa Harrop, Sean Harris

Chapter summary

Schools which authentically tackle poverty and champion social justice do this at a whole-school level. In this chapter, we explore some of the ways in which this can be done.

What does the research suggest?

Extensive research highlights the importance of building school cultures that foster belonging and promote social justice. This section outlines key studies that have shaped our understanding of creating equitable environments for children, young people, staff and communities.

These insights have helped leaders and teachers move beyond charitable acts to cultivate a deeper commitment to tackling inequality within their schools and local contexts.

Research 1

Berkowitz et al. (2016)

'A research synthesis of the associations between socioeconomic background, inequality, school climate, and academic achievement'

This review of research studies examines whether a positive school climate can successfully disrupt the associations between low income and limited academic achievement.

Berkowitz et al. suggest that school climate can mitigate some poverty-related barriers to learning. They suggest that schools promoting a positive climate and equality can help to tackle socioeconomic inequalities and enable greater social mobility.

Key points

Practical suggestions offered through the research review include:

- Involve different members of the school community in helping to formulate the school vision and values. This needs to be more than simply school leaders and governors (e.g. pupils, parents, local community representatives).
- Involve school community members in considering the type of school climate that they want, and regularly review the school values. For example, invite pupils to consider what the school values mean in action and where they can see them practised.
- Support school leaders to understand and take part in research that shows how school climate has improved over time. For example, sharing best-practice examples of work taking place in schools to promote a positive climate for learning but which cannot be easily measured in the same way as other school improvement initiatives (e.g. improving attendance).
- Encourage school leaders to use focus groups to research school climate and how it is understood by pupils, teachers and other stakeholders. Examples to further develop this are explored in Chapter 14.

Research 2

Baars et al. (2018)

'School cultures and practices: Supporting the attainment of disadvantaged pupils: A qualitative comparison of London and non-London schools'

This research is based on in-depth case studies of primary and secondary schools across England. Baars et al. provide an analysis of a set of school cultures and practices that correlate to positive outcomes for pupils facing poverty-related barriers to learning. These cultures and practices range from how schools support parent and pupil expectations to the way in which data is used to analyse pupil performance.

Examples include:

- placing emphasis on the quality of support staff
- recruiting staff who share the school's ethos
- providing a variety of community partnerships to deliver extra-curricular activities

- habitually celebrating pupil achievements
- engaging parents with the school's ethos and vision.

Key points

- Schools with lower impact on attainment appeared to have less developed strategies for engaging and helping parents support disadvantaged pupils at home.
- These same schools appeared less likely to believe that disadvantaged pupils can achieve in line with all other pupils.

Research 3

Cummins and Di Prato (2021)

A School for Tomorrow: 'The character issue'

CIRCLE, the Centre for Innovation, Research, Creativity and Leadership in Education, is a division of A School for Tomorrow, a global educational network dedicated to supporting pupils, teachers and leaders.

Their primary aim is to enhance character education and leadership strategies to ensure that schools evolve into stronger places of belonging and purpose. Through a variety of research publications and training sessions, CIRCLE assists school leaders in understanding how social justice and community advocacy can be achieved through robust character education.

The research conducted by CIRCLE outlines several important themes.

- **Value of character and wellness:** Character, competency and wellness are identified as the hallmark of a school that is prepared for the future. This approach focuses on the overall development of pupils, ensuring that they are equipped with the necessary skills and values to thrive.
- **Support and challenge:** Schools should ensure that pupils are empowered through a balanced approach of challenge and support as central to their education.
- **Conditions for agency:** The research highlights the importance of setting conditions that allow for greater personalisation and pupil agency. This personalised approach is fundamental to effective learning and the holistic growth of each child, ensuring that education is tailored to meet individual needs and ambitions.

Key points

- Cummins and Di Prato (2021) explain that character and school culture are closely linked throughout the learning experience. The report highlights the importance of school leaders working with pupils and other stakeholders to define what 'character' means. This definition should be supported by real-world examples so that everyone in the school understands and accepts it.
- Schools need to describe what a meaningful and well-lived life looks like from their community's perspective, in order to decide on the character traits they want to develop in their pupils.
- Cummins and Di Prato also emphasise that character development is a shared responsibility for schools. Everyone in the school community plays a part in making sure the character education programme is comprehensive and deeply integrated into the school's culture.

Research 4

Forde et al. (2021)

'Caring practices and social justice leadership: case studies of school principals in Scotland and USA'

This research explores how school leaders develop social justice in their daily work, using case studies from Scottish and American research in the International School Leadership Development Network (ISLDN). An ISLDN project on social justice leadership explored four main questions about how leaders in education understand social justice, what supports or hinders their work, and how they develop personally.

Researchers conducted case studies in Scotland and Tennessee, selecting headteachers and principals known locally for their efforts in promoting equality and social justice in their communities. Researchers used in-depth interviews during which participants reflected on their own beliefs and values and talked about the practical actions they take to promote social justice in their schools. From these interviews, researchers identified key themes and created a detailed report that includes profiles of each school involved in the study.

In creating genuinely inclusive school environments, the everyday actions of school leaders are crucial. They play a vital role in challenging small forms of discrimination and subtle insults (micro-aggressions) that can make diverse pupils feel unwelcome. The research looks closely at 'leadership practice' through the idea of relational leadership, which highlights the personal interactions and relationships that shape leadership. It explores caring behaviours like setting a good example, having open conversations and giving supportive feedback.

Key points

- School leaders can effectively promote social justice by focusing on setting clear goals and values as they build trust amongst the school community. These elements are crucial for promoting fairness and inclusivity.

- Social justice can be further achieved by school leaders actively engaging with their school community through listening, collaborating and fostering trust. This approach helps leaders and other colleagues to be responsive to issues of inequality when they occur.

- Small acts of kindness and fairness from school leaders can make a big difference in how pupils and staff feel at school.

- Effective leadership for social justice involves combining practical management with personal support to create positive conditions for change – for example, offering personal support to colleagues on implementation of ideas and managing change in schools.

- The individual needs of pupils and staff are understood as an important part of achieving conditions for social justice. This balance creates supportive school environments in which everyone can learn and thrive.

Other useful research

- **Arthur et al. (2017) A habit of service** – This research shows that young people engaged in multiple types of service activities, such as contributing to social justice initiatives, were more inclined to develop a consistent habit of service. The study advocates for those involved in working with children and young people to actively promote regular opportunities for children to engage in serving others and their communities. Additionally, sharing stories of social action is encouraged as a means to inspire others and make participation in such activities a regular part of promoting social justice.

- **Flutter (2007):** The contribution of pupil voice to school improvement: this paper explores how effective pupil voice not only contributes to teacher development but also helps to create more inclusive and equitable educational environments. By amplifying pupil voice and involving pupils in decision-making, schools can potentially address disparities, promote fairness and improve educational outcomes for all pupils.

- **Ridge (2011):** The Everyday Cost of Poverty in Childhood – this study reviews qualitative research to uncover the day-to-day challenges and struggles faced by children from low-income families. It explores how poverty as a social injustice affects various aspects of the lives of children, but does this through the voice and eyes of children themselves. It is a useful study for showing how social injustice can be better understood and tackled by directly listening to those impacted by injustice.

Research takeaways

- Schools that authentically champion social justice do this at a whole-school level.
- Social justice can be further achieved by school leaders actively engaging with their school community by listening, collaborating and fostering trust. This approach helps leaders and other colleagues to be responsive to issues of inequality when they occur.
- Ensuring that the individual needs of pupils and staff in school communities are understood is an important part of achieving conditions for social justice.
- Listening carefully to pupil voice and involving pupils in decision-making can help schools to address disparities, promote fairness and improve educational outcomes.
- An effective school culture can help to facilitate greater relationships between adults and pupils, participation in social justice and a commitment to community.
- Involving pupils in regular opportunities for service to others and championing social justice can help to form a habit of service to others.

Beith Primary School – core values

Following discussions with pupils, staff and parent focus groups, the school identified three core values (nurture, respect, inspire) that permeate their policies as a school community. Pupils reflect on these values every week and awards presented in assemblies are based on these values.

The school describes itself as a 'Rights Respecting School' and uses various charters across the school community written in consultation with children and families. A Rights Respecting School, accredited by the United Nations International Children's Emergency Fund (UNICEF), guides teachers and staff through a transformative journey lasting up to four years. It provides training, resources and assessments by child rights professionals, supporting schools to integrate children's rights into daily practice. This initiative not only educates pupils on global issues such as climate change and refugee crises, but also fosters a collaborative environment where children and adults work together to promote and uphold rights, benefiting children's wellbeing, participation, relationships and self-esteem, with a positive impact extending beyond the school community. Beith is accredited as a Gold Level Rights Respecting School. Children's rights are at the heart of all learning and teaching at Beith Primary School.

The school also supports pupils in understanding about social injustices such as racism, poverty and other forms of disadvantage. One example is a lunchtime charter that children have produced to demonstrate a commitment to ensuring all members of the school have access to nutritious food and feel valued.

Beith Primary: Lunchtime charter
We all have the right to: • nutritious food • a clean environment • clean water • feel safe.

This is how we can respect these rights in our school:
- Eat all of our food.
- Put waste in the recycling bins.
- Always remember our manners.
- Wash our hands before we eat.
- Use an indoor voice.
- Keep calm.
- Respect everyone – adults and children.

 Ideas to try

Read the signs

Even before visitors or pupils enter a school building, the external-facing communications of a school community can help to convey a school's culture. Consider the extent to which the school logo, signage and messaging demonstrate the mission and values of the school. Reflect on how these demonstrate a commitment to the community, local identity and social justice.

Suggestions

Examples of questions to consider might include:

- Are the school values clear to all stakeholders? (E.g. do the values make sense to children, families and all adults working in the school?)

- To what extent can stakeholders explain what the values of the school mean in practice?

- How do the mission and values of the school demonstrate that every child and adult matters?

- To what extent do the mission and values of the school celebrate and champion diversity?

- In what ways are the local context of the school community reflected in the mission and values of the school? (E.g. a commitment to local identity, heritage or issues that are important for the local community.)

- How often are the mission and values revisited and revised with pupils, families, staff and other stakeholders?

Championing charity

Actively engaging in charity and social action projects is something that many schools will regularly do. It is important that these are implemented effectively to have a meaningful and purposeful impact.

Suggestions

- Before or after a fundraising event for a local charity, consider activities such as inviting a spokesperson from the charity to share the work of the charity and how the resources will be used. Pupils could be tasked with finding out about the charity as part of a research project and presenting different aspects of its work to other pupils (e.g. case studies of how the charity has supported others, how people can actively support the work of the charity). This could help pupils to develop a sense of commitment to a local charity and further understand their work in their local neighbourhood.

- Consider the extent to which pupils and families are involved in selecting charitable causes that matter to their community. This might include inviting pupils to research different charities, as outlined above, and then presenting their findings to each other, with the challenge of having to select one that the pupils will commit to fundraising for. Examples of local charities could be promoted in a school magazine or via social media, with the invitation for families to vote for the charity that they would like the school to commit to working with more in future. This might lead to some families involved with the charity sharing their own story or providing links for direct contact with charities or particular projects.

- Clear links could be made with local or regional charities as part of learning about social justice in areas of the curriculum. For example, when learning about the Islamic tradition of *zakah* (giving money to charity), we often invite pupils to find examples of charities that local Muslims provide money to and which uphold the Islamic belief in serving others.

- It is important to consider the voices of children as part of social justice and community action, as outlined in the research section of this chapter. In one school that we work with, pupils challenged a decision to get involved in an international charity project that sends Christmas items to children overseas. Pupils explained that whilst they could see the value of international need, they also wanted to do something that would regularly support local children and families in their own neighbourhood.

Signpost social justice

In our work with schools in disadvantaged contexts, we have found that families often appreciate schools making an effort to signpost support for low-income households. This has been especially important through times of economic hardship. Social media, newsletters and routine communications to families are a good way of signalling support and a commitment to social justice.

Suggestions

Examples might include:

- Signpost examples of low-income or free activities in academic holidays and in the local area, remembering that not all families have access to cars.
- Provide recipes that support cooking on a budget.
- Facilitate campaigns that encourage families to give to local causes (e.g. foodbank support). Be careful with the wording so as not to add pressure to low-income families.
- Organise surveys that encourage families to indicate what local needs there are.
- Provide free buy-or-borrow-shops that do not pressure families to donate (e.g. uniform, PE kits or reusable study materials such as revision books).

Grow social justice networks

Consider forming partnerships with national education networks and charities.

SHINE

Each year, the charity SHINE runs the 'Let Teachers Shine' campaign to fund innovation from teachers for a project that aims to tackle disadvantage in their school. See the links at the end of the chapter for more information about the work of SHINE and projects it has launched. Working with this charity has enabled schools in Tees Valley Education Trust to develop a project aimed at supporting teachers in designing curriculum approaches to tackle poverty-related barriers to learning in classrooms. School leaders and teachers are actively encouraged to apply for this funding, as it helps to enable schools to further support innovation on tackling educational inequality.

In collaboration with partners such as the Steve Morgan Foundation, UBS Optimus Foundation, Wirral Council and Right to Succeed, SHINE has played a pivotal role in the Cradle to Career initiative in North Birkenhead. This project places residents at the centre of educational services and decision-making processes. Over three years, significant strides have been made within the education component of the initiative: eight schools have shown progress, with four exceeding expected benchmarks and the remaining four meeting expectations. There has been a notable shift towards higher reading proficiency, evidenced by a 42 per cent increase in high-ability readers and a five per cent decrease in those needing the most reading support. Furthermore, 467 pupils across Years 1, 2 and 3 have improved their reading skills to a level that predicts they will achieve more than half a GCSE grade higher in every subject. This collective effort highlights SHINE's commitment to fostering educational improvement and equity in North Birkenhead. It also provides a genuine example of place-based change in communities and tackling inequality at scale.

Fair Education Alliance (FEA)

The FEA is another organisation that supports establishment to understand and tackle educational disadvantage at scale. FEA leverages the expertise of over 300 member organisations across the UK to share best practice and collective action and access CPD to support the tackling of educational inequality. In addition to facilitating collective action and influencing policy, the FEA engages in a range of activities to advance its mission. This includes conducting research and advocating for policies that promote fair education outcomes. The FEA also forms partnerships with educational institutions and government bodies to strengthen its impact. Community engagement plays a crucial role, involving stakeholders to raise awareness and mobilise support for equitable education practices.

In addition, members are actively encouraged to apply for funding that can be used to generate ideas and projects in schools for tackling causes of inequality. Every year, the FEA facilitates a summit event that invites organisations and individuals dedicated to tackling inequality and system change. This is an excellent opportunity for school leaders and other organisations to share and learn from best practice. In Chapter 11, you can explore more ways to grow professional partnerships to tackle poverty and disadvantage at scale.

Invest in people

Developing and equipping teachers to serve local communities is vital.

Suggestions

- **Understand local need and context:** This is explored in the opening chapters in greater depth. It is important to help school leaders to understand and apply data that can help to describe local need. Explore local income deprivation (available through the Office of National Statistics) and reports such as the annual Poverty UK reports (available through the Joseph Rowntree Foundation) as a helpful starting point.
- **Communication and pupil relations support:** Support teachers, especially those new to the profession, with understanding the needs of local families, and provide CPD opportunities to develop effective communication skills. This is especially important in developing communication channels with the community (e.g. newsletters, websites or social media posts).
- **Support expertise development:** Provide timely reminders and opportunities for colleagues to get involved in local charities. Some schools provide opportunities for teachers to serve as a governor in other schools to help make a commitment to the wider community.

Rights Respecting Schools

It is important to consider the extent to which school culture, policies and processes demonstrate a commitment to equal rights and the rights of children. The case study in this chapter gives an example of this in action.

Recruitment and induction

Staff recruitment and induction is an important part of cultivating a commitment to social justice.

Suggestions

- Ask candidates to research and demonstrate an understanding of local poverty or different facets of disadvantage that pupils might face (e.g. ask candidates to prepare a presentation about a specific barrier to learning/challenge that they think local pupils will face and how they might help to tackle it).

- Design intentional opportunities for teachers to meet with pupils and families to understand the context that the school serves (e.g. inviting new members of staff to shadow parental engagement meetings between pastoral staff and parents/carers).
- Actively invite parents or local community representatives to support with recruitment and relevant CPD where appropriate to do so.

Temperature-check culture

Ensure that families, pupils and all school staff are actively involved in helping to temperature-check the culture and ethos of the school.

Suggestions

- Conduct regular surveys and focus group discussions.
- Some of our schools routinely host parental coffee mornings to ensure that local families have an opportunity to have a hot drink and meet with staff informally in school to discuss any issues, challenges or concerns. As part of these discussions, families are asked to comment on what the school is doing well and where the school culture can be developed.

Talking poverty

You can sense-check a commitment to social justice by exploring with leaders how the concepts of social justice and poverty are talked about and understood by the whole school community. For example, in many church schools, leaders might demonstrate a commitment to social justice as part of their school's mission statement.

Suggestions

- **Develop a common language of justice:** Ensure that these concepts are regularly talked about and understood, not just in lesson curriculum time but also through other activities such as tutor time, assemblies or school newsletters. In church schools we have worked with, leaders have looked at how children can make links between regular activities that take place in the school and theological concepts such as stewardship and helping others.

- **Displays that focus on specific examples of social justice in action:** This can help the school community make links between social justice and specific projects that the school has co-ordinated with the community.

- **Ethos days:** Build event days around facets of social injustice that pupils recognise as something that they want to challenge. This might include aspects of poverty or, more broadly, examples of hate crime, societal injustice or responses to international issues that impact disadvantaged communities. In one school that we work with, sixth-formers were involved in designing two days a year in which pupils would learn about specific injustices and issues that mattered to them. One of the days consisted of sixth form pupils learning about the risks of extremism in the modern world and interviewing a range of religious and political figures from the local community about the work that they do to tackle extremism in their communities. Pupils also had the opportunity to meet with a victim of hate crime, who outlined to pupils the personal impact of discrimination and how it impacts communities.

Chapter takeaways

- Consider the extent to which the whole community is actively involved in helping to temperature-check the culture and ethos of the school.
- Recruitment and professional development of all staff is an important way of building a school culture committed to social justice.
- Partnership with charities, organisations and local community representatives is vital. Schools do not achieve social justice in isolation.
- Design school communications, curriculum and opportunities to intentionally champion causes that the community care about.

Recap and Reflective tasks

Recap

Indicate which statements are true or false based on your understanding.	True	False
School culture is unlikely to tackle barriers to learning related to poverty.		
Developing pupil advocacy can further contribute to pupils having a greater sense of belonging in schools and improved relationships between pupils and adults.		
A school's culture can be measured in the same way that attainment and attendance data are measured. There is a clear formula to it.		
Research indicates that the success of an agreed ethos for character education begins with working out what schools mean by character.		

Reflective tasks

Reflective task for leaders and teacher educators
• What is your school vision and mission statement? (Recall it by memory if you can initially.) • To what extent is social justice evident in your school vision and values? • How is this conveyed through the logo, values or external messaging of the school?

Leadership reflection Sit with a group of other leaders and/or teacher educators in your school(s). Invite them to each complete the above activity. Then consider and summarise:	
What injustices are evident in our local or regional context as a school?	Which aspects of our vision statement and values address these?

Consider and summarise the ways in which social justice is championed through:
Teacher education/CPD programmes
Appointment and induction processes for staff
Classroom ethos and climate

School behaviour, sanctions and rewards policies
Curriculum narrative and intent
Wider/extra-curricular opportunities for pupils and families in the community

Reflective task for teachers/curriculum leaders
• Consider specific examples of injustice that are important in your context. • Where are the opportunities to learn about and unpack these issues in terms of:

Curriculum subjects/topics	Assembly/reflection time	Wider/extra-curricular activities

Next, consider both the learning and action that can underpin pupil experience of this topic.

What do pupils learn about these issue(s)?	What opportunities do pupils have to act on this by way of commitment to social justice?
E.g. global warming: in geography, pupils learn about the ways in which the climate crisis can be better responded to by businesses and politicians.	*E.g. pupils write letters in English to local MPs to campaign around environmental action.*

Example:

Imagine that the school has implemented a new charity week. All pupils in the school will be actively involved in promoting and raising money for a charity of their choosing as part of a commitment to social action. Consider the topics explored so far in this chapter and other chapters.

What might be the barriers to this for some pupils in your classroom with experience of poverty?

How could your subject(s)/curriculum be used to help access learning about a specific charity?

How could your classroom culture support learning about this charity/ social justice without pupils feeling further disadvantaged in this project? Consider:		
Local need How could pupils be involved in identifying the charity or a social justice cause close to them?	Knowledge What could be taught about the charity? In the project?	Method How might pupils practically be involved without giving money?

📖 Further reading

Ambrose et al. (2010) – *How Learning Works: Seven Research-Based Principles for Smart Teaching*

Andrews et al. (2017) – 'Closing the gap? Trends in educational attainment and disadvantage'

Cambron-McCabe and McCarthy (2005) – 'Educating school leaders for social justice'

Smith (2015) – *Mentoring At-Risk Pupils Through the Hidden Curriculum of Higher Education*

Walton, and Cohen (2011) – 'A brief social-belonging intervention improves academic and health outcomes of minority pupils'

Links

A School for Tomorrow.: www.aschoolfortomorrow.com
SHINE: www.shinetrust.org.uk/what-we-do/let-teachers-shine
Fair Education Alliance (FEA): www.faireducation.org.uk
Office for National Statistics: www.ons.gov.uk

9 Reading and literacy
Sean Harris, Katrina Morley

Chapter summary

Living in poverty does not determine a pupil's ability to read, nor their overall academic achievement. However, extensive research suggests that many pupils from low-income backgrounds face increased challenges in reading, including difficulties in decoding text and comprehending it.

Barriers can include but are not limited to:

- poor access to quality reading books due to the cost of materials
- lack of access to local libraries or up-to-date stocks of reading materials
- lack of access to an environment where books can be read quietly or independently
- limited reading or literacy skills of adults in the home environment
- underdeveloped phonological awareness or understanding.

The topics of teaching reading and supporting pupils to read in schools are explored more extensively in other literature. In this chapter, we focus on some of the research regarding poverty and the links to reading outcomes. We outline some best-practice examples of how school leaders and teachers have responded to a range of barriers in their settings.

 What does the research suggest?

There is a vast amount of research into the development of reading in schools and there are books covering effective approaches to teaching reading skills and knowledge in detail. In this section, we provide a sample of the research that we have found helpful in understanding correlations between poverty-related barriers to learning and reading.

Research 1

National Literacy Trust: Picton and Clark (2023)

'Children and young people's book ownership in 2023: A 10-year retrospective'

The National Literacy Trust (NLT) produces annual research examining literacy and reading habits in the UK. These show distinct correlations between poverty, disadvantage and literacy levels in communities.

The annual book ownership survey is helpful for schools wanting to understand national trends in how poverty can impact access to crucial materials needed to build literacy skills and good reading habits. It suggests that with mounting pressure on household budgets as a result of socioeconomic disadvantage, barriers to anything other than essential – survival – spend is being created.

In the annual report 2023, it was reported that the cost-of-living crisis had a direct impact on families' ability to support reading at home. More than one in three (36 per cent) of parents struggling financially indicated that they were buying fewer books for their children compared to previous years. Moreover, the percentage of eight- to 18-year-olds who own at least one book has fallen to its lowest level in five years.

Key points

- In 2023, one in eight (12.4 per cent) of eight- to 18-year-olds receiving FSM indicated they did not have a book of their own compared to the previous year.
- This is double the percentage of their peers who did not receive FSM (12.4 per cent versus 5.8 per cent).
- The percentage-point (pp) gap in book ownership between children and young people who receive FSM and their peers who do not (6.6 pp) is the largest in a decade.
- This research is helpful for challenging the view that all families with a low income somehow lack a desire or aspiration to read – it is about limited access, as opposed to a lack of willingness to engage in reading.

Research 2

Dolean et al. (2019)

'Achievement gap: Socioeconomic status affects reading development beyond language and cognition in children facing poverty'

Numerous studies show moderate to high links between income status, reading access and reading abilities. This particular study is useful for understanding how socioeconomic status can be related to the development of reading skills in children facing severe and intersectional poverty. It also suggests that this is compounded over a lifetime.

The study tracked over 300 Roma children facing severe poverty and compared them to other groups of children. Roma children in the study had limited initial reading and a slower growth of their reading skills.

Key points

- Socioeconomic status has a strong impact on children's early reading skills and their subsequent development.

- Socioeconomic status negatively affects school absence. In turn, this impacts upon the access to language development.

- Teaching and intervention should focus on mastering early reading skills as quickly as possible.

- Schools should also focus on family engagement with literature and the reading process.

Research 3

Kellet and Dar (2007)

'Children researching links between poverty and literacy'

Whilst small in sample size, this research is powerfully led by children. It includes details of their own experiences and lived reality, which will help schools to see the associative impact between disadvantage and reading through the eyes of their children. It also begins to highlight the power of children as researchers and contributors in their own right to the evidence base across education. (This is covered in more detail in Chapter 14.)

Key points

The research has some notable findings:

- Children from lower socioeconomic backgrounds can have less confidence about their reading and writing abilities.
- They are also less likely to have routine support for their homework, including quiet, personal spaces and a range of materials and resources.
- Therefore, considering how you can offer the children in your school some personal space and support may help to improve their reading confidence and their subsequent literacy levels.

Other useful research

- **Cremin et al. (2009):** This research suggests that creating a positive reading culture in school, including reading for pleasure, can increase motivation for reading for all children, including those who struggle.
- **Gay et al. (2021):** This study highlights the need to consider both home and school influences on children's reading skills, as both environments have an impact on language acquisition and development.
- **Quigley and Coleman (2021):** This guidance report, produced by the EEF, aims to help secondary schools improve literacy in different subject areas. It provides seven recommendations related to reading, writing, talk, vocabulary development and supporting struggling pupils. It demonstrates that English teaching in secondary schools is the responsibility of all departments and subject areas.

Research takeaways

- Research indicates that reading difficulties are amplified for many pupils and families living in poverty and facing disadvantage.
- Poverty presents additional barriers in and out of school that can impact the extent to which pupils have access to books and a range of reading materials.

- When trying to raise literacy levels and reading abilities, it is important to promote reading as a pleasurable and accessible experience.
- Other intersectional dimensions of poverty, such as subject-specific homework support and quiet spaces to work in, need to be considered when understanding barriers to reading and tackling poverty in schools.

 Case Study

Lea Forest Primary Academy – Developing a love of reading in school and the local community

Craig Clarke-Castello

Listen to families

We regularly listen to families and encourage parents to speak to us about reading, through routine coffee mornings and parental surveys. This helps us to get an understanding of current barriers to reading and questions that families have about access to books, reading skills and texts we provide children with.

Book vending machines

Every week, pupils nominated as star learners visit our book vending machines and choose a book to keep and read. These are refurbished drinks vending machines that we accessed with the help of local organisations. Our pupils take great pleasure in taking their token from prize-giving assemblies and selecting their own books from the vending machines in the reception area of the academy. The vending machines are one of the first things that children and families visiting the school see when they walk through our doors. It reminds them that reading is at the heart of our academy.

Curriculum intent

Our curriculum intent for reading is simple: all pupils need to be supported to develop a love of reading. This is essential if they are to access concepts, topics and complex narratives made available in all other curriculum areas. Reading is the gateway to every other subject. Each subject area is given dedicated planning time for reading. Phase and subject leaders also have access to bespoke CPD to understand how to implement effective reading in their areas.

Voices of pupils

Pupils are your main stakeholders in schools. Reading is something we want every child to enjoy and have an interest in; this is especially important for pupils facing poverty and disadvantage. We have a Junior Leadership Team (JLT) who have reading as one of their main priority areas. The JLT meet regularly with senior leaders to talk about issues related to reading and how the school can support more children to have access to books. Our JLT worked with the headteacher and other leaders to co-design the library, revise its opening times and celebrate the use of it on social media. Our pupils have a real sense of ownership in their reading provision.

Reader of the week

Every week, a pupil is nominated in each class by a teacher and other pupils as the 'Reader of the Week'. We challenge pupils and teachers to look beyond reading ability as the criteria for this recognition. Instead, we focus on those who have shown motivation for reading, who have tried reading something different to their usual reading habits or who have made progress in particular reading habits. The nominated pupils can take home a reading suitcase. This contains books recommended by other pupils and activities for the pupil to complete with their families. Pupils are encouraged to write a review of the book and we provide hot chocolate sachets for them to enjoy with families. This helps to reinforce the view that snuggling up with a hot drink and a good book is a great habit.

 Ideas to try

In all schools, both teachers and pupils should have ample opportunities to interact with and be surrounded by language-rich environments, with a particular emphasis on reading. This becomes especially crucial within disadvantaged communities. In this section, we offer practical suggestions on how leaders and teachers can develop these opportunities within schools.

Begin with barriers to reading

Identify the specific barriers that might exist to reading and literacy for pupils in your school that face poverty-related barriers to learning. Also focus on those children and young people who are struggling with reading or displaying a lack of enthusiasm for reading, to identify specific barriers and strategies to overcome them. Carefully consider the extent to which pupil and parent/carer voices are involved here. Finally, think about where you provide regular and timely opportunities for pupils to engage with texts, in a range of formats, to read for both meaning and pleasure.

For example, in one school that we work with, pupils in a reluctant readers group are encouraged to routinely share where they find it easy and difficult to read. This helps teachers understand how to better facilitate access to reading. One pupil commented to teachers that they found it hard to concentrate at home when reading because of the sound of motorbikes outside their bedroom window. Another pupil shared that they only read one particular author because these were the books they could afford in the local supermarket. These deeply personal reflections need to be considered when planning the reading curriculum pathways, to ensure access to reading for all.

Practical considerations

Also consider:

- **Access to a range of reading materials and books:** Use the annual research from NLT and other sources to gauge an understanding of the access to texts that pupils have and how financial hardship can limit this.
- **Library access and closures:** Gaining an understanding of local library provision and trends in library use can also be helpful for understanding local access to books and reading. This can help schools to inform what might additionally be needed in schools or through extra-curricular activities.

Reading basics

Get back to basics: every pupil needs to be able to read. To do this they must have access to texts, and this is especially important for pupils facing barriers to reading and learning as a result of poverty. Some of the key principles to check and consider in schools as part of a reading and learning strategy include:

Phonics

Phonics programmes are important, but so too is the rigour of monitoring and evaluation that sits around them. Pupils struggling with decoding need ongoing phonic development opportunities. Evaluate the extent to which all teachers are supported in developing an understanding of phonics and supporting phonological awareness in schools and across all subjects. This is not simply an area of focus for primary schools but needs to be considered for secondary school pupils and other education settings.

Complex vocabulary

It is important to identify and consider how to teach complex vocabulary across all subjects. If pupils are encountering concepts or words for the first time, then they will struggle with not only decoding the words but also understanding subject-specific vocabulary.

Support teachers with identifying which complex concepts and associated complex vocabulary need to be taught and ensure that pupils are routinely over-exposed to these through the curriculum.

Reading spine

Consider the reading journey you want pupils to undertake, from their first years in the school to the later stages and beyond. This should be understood by teachers and pupils, so explain why these books have been chosen, why they are important as part of the overall reading journey and how they facilitate access to learning and life.

Developing a culture of reading

Whilst many pupils need encouragement to read for pleasure, pupils facing poverty and disadvantage often need extra support and regular access to these opportunities. Expecting pupils in these circumstances to simply read in the same way as their more affluent peers is unrealistic.

These are some strategies that schools might want to use to support all children to become readers:

Hyperlocal reading associations

Giving pupils an understanding of either local authors or books set locally can help forge real-life connections, celebrate place and allow all children insight into the link between their life and books.

In many of our schools, we have found local authors to be hugely supportive of working directly with pupils, in understanding their work and in celebrating local place, colloquialisms or traits, through reading. This has engaged more children and inspired them to read more, as well as offering families an opportunity to discuss the book and areas, thus engaging with their child's reading. You can also encourage this familial and community-based approach through partnerships and visits with local bookshops.

Library stock

Ensure that library areas are well-stocked. Involve pupils in managing and selecting a range of texts and books for these spaces. Routine opportunities for whole classes to visit the library areas and spend time in independent reading with texts that they enjoy is essential to ensuring pupils understand the value of libraries too. In primary schools, this might extend to local library visits to support pupils in understanding how to access and make use of library services with families.

Author visits and collaborations

Many authors are willing to work with schools as a means of promoting their work but to also champion a love of reading. This is not exclusive to primary schools. Consider inviting local businesses, bookshops and charities to sponsor these events or to purchase books that can be signed and shared with all pupils as part of the event.

Staff reading

Encouraging all adults in schools to celebrate their reading habits and choice of texts might further help to promote a love of reading. Add favourite books and what staff are reading to office doors, signature lines on emails and through school newsletters. Use this as an opportunity to celebrate a diversity of reading for pleasure habits and preferences.

Links to other events

Consider how reading can be championed through other whole-school, whole-trust, local area and national events.

For example, as part of mental health day, one of our schools encourages pupils to learn about the ways in which reading can support mental health and wellbeing.

Another reading investment is the 'Tees Valley Education book of the year' competition, where children vote on their favourite text, having accessed four across the year. Authors are invited to the end-of-year ceremony along with children, families and staff. This is supported by a local independent book store, whose team are deeply committed to every child having a book.

World Book Day

World Book Day is an annual event that is celebrated in schools and organisations globally. Whilst it is vitally important to celebrate a love of reading in schools, it is just as important to consider the added pressures and hidden costs that might exist in celebratory events for pupils and families with low income. This is explored in further detail in Chapter 3.

Consider options with no hidden costs:

- Decorate their tutor room or classroom door in the theme of a book.
- Collect the physical books with the tokens that are given to each child and give them out in school, so the children can go home with a book in their hand and not a token.
- Invite book clubs into the school so that the children can spend the tokens themselves within the school environment, and don't need their parents to have access to transport to get anywhere.

Chapter takeaways

- It is important for teachers and leaders to understand specific contextual and life barriers to reading that exist for all pupils but especially those facing poverty and disadvantage.
- Identify where the gaps are for pupils in relation to reading provision. Library closures and limited stock of books will likely provide even further barriers for those in low-income contexts.

Reading and literacy

- Ensure that teachers and leaders understand, consistently teach and regularly revisit the fundamentals of your reading curriculum (e.g. phonics or complex vocabulary).
- Support teachers across all subjects in understanding and applying the basics of reading across multiple phases and curriculum areas.
- Find cost-effective alternatives when organising celebratory book events. This helps to foster an inclusive love of reading for all pupils, without exarcebating further inequalities.

Recap and Reflective tasks

Recap

Indicate which statements are true or false based on your understanding.	True	False
Research indicates that reading difficulties increase for many pupils and families as a result of poverty and disadvantage.		
Research suggests that poverty mostly causes the same barriers to learning for pupils in reading as it does across other learning skills and subjects.		
Attempts to tackle barriers to reading in secondary schools should solely be implemented through teachers of English and literacy.		
Schools should ban or remove celebratory reading events and activities to remove added pressures on low-income families and pupils.		

Reflective tasks

Reflective task for leaders and teacher educators
• What are your main takeaways from this chapter?

Leadership reflection

Work with a range of leaders when considering these tasks. You might do this independently and then compare your reflections.

What are the specific barriers to reading/books that exist in your school related to poverty?	How do you know this? What evidence supports this?

What are your current and main approaches to tackling these barriers?

Reflective task for teachers/curriculum leaders

• How do poverty and disadvantage impact reading for pupils?
• Summarise your main takeaways from this chapter.

Understanding poverty and reading in your subject/classroom

How does poverty impact reading and therefore accessibility to your subject?

What are some of the ways in which this is addressed through:	
Whole-school/other subject intervention	Your subject/classroom

What research has been used to help inform these strategies?	
Internal evidence (e.g. within school)	External evidence (e.g. EEF, research papers)

Developing a reading culture	
In what ways could a love of reading be further championed through your subject/phase?	What support do you/other teachers in your subject/phase need to further develop a reading culture? E.g. understanding barriers of specific pupils, phonics training…

 Further reading

Joseph Rowntree Foundation (2023) – 'What is poverty?'

Links

National Literacy Trust: https://literacytrust.org.uk
World Book Day: www.worldbookday.com

PART 3

Tackling poverty in other ways

10 Tackling the cycle of exclusion

Martyn Gordon, Sean Harris

Chapter summary

In this chapter, we look at some of the research that explains how poverty and school exclusion can be linked. We also consider some practical approaches that schools can consider in tackling school exclusion and poverty.

What does the research suggest?

Various studies have highlighted increases in school permanent exclusions and fixed-term exclusion (FTE) suspensions. Some studies suggest that Black pupils, pupils facing disadvantage and pupils with SEND represent a concerning number of the pupils excluded from mainstream education (DfE, 2019; Demie, 2022; Timpson, 2019; Child of the North, 2024). In this section, we summarise some of the research that has been helpful to us as leaders in mainstream and in alternative provision (AP) schools.

Research 1

Gazeley (2012)

'The impact of social class on parent-professional interaction in school exclusion processes: Deficit or disadvantage?'
Louise Gazeley is Professor of Educational and Social Disadvantage based in the School of Education and Social Work (ESW) at the University of Sussex. This study explores school exclusion processes and the ways in which family income might shape families' interactions with schools. Exclusion processes are demanding for families and schools, and parents have to negotiate complex formal processes. This study highlights the complexities that low-income status can add to the process.

Key points

- Social class and income status impact parental–school relationships and interactions during formal exclusion processes.

- In some incidents, low-income parents were less articulate and persuasive than other families.

- Parents indicated feeling ineffective and solely responsible for all of the barriers faced by their child.

- Some parents suggested that this was compounded by a feeling that the school rarely shared positive recognition for their child's achievements.

Research 2

Demie (2022)

Understanding the Causes and Consequences of School Exclusions: Teachers, Parents and Schools' Perspectives

Feyisa Demie is an honorary professor at Durham University's School of Education and the Head of Research and Adviser for School Self-Evaluation at Lambeth Local Authority. He has collaborated extensively with local authorities, government departments and schools to utilise research and data for school improvement. This book by Demie looks at the causes and consequences of school exclusions and highlights intersectional aspects of disadvantage, such as the experience of minority ethnic pupils and those with SEND. Demie examines different exclusion methods in schools, such as fixed-term, informal, internal exclusions, 'off-rolling' and permanent exclusions, moving beyond the simpler terms of 'suspension' and 'exclusion'. The book draws on a range of research and literature to better understand how these issues are central to public and educational policy debates in England, and explores the rise in exclusion rates due to education system fragmentation, funding cuts and other factors impacting the sector.

Key points

- Factors associated with rises in school exclusions across the UK include league-table pressures on school leaders, austerity and significant funding cuts in education.

- Increasing numbers of children are living in poverty. This, combined with other factors, has contributed to increases in school exclusions. Demie cites factors such as funding cuts, the rise of the education market, informal off-rolling to improve GCSE results and a lack of diversity in the school workforces.

- High proportions of pupils with SEND and pupils facing disadvantage being excluded can be linked to multiple factors, including institutional racism, unconscious bias and a lack of understanding about specific poverty-related barriers to learning.

Research 3

Gill et al. (2017)

'Making The Difference: Breaking the link between school exclusion and social exclusion'

Gill et al. argue that schools should prioritise addressing exclusions, which makes sense both economically and socially for the UK. Their report supports the creation of The Difference, an organisation dedicated to developing specialist school leaders who can combat social exclusion in schools.

Key points

Gill et al. note a range of factors that are useful in understanding the link between social exclusion and school exclusions:

- Some pupils are unofficially excluded, which means that the exclusion problem is arguably bigger than the official exclusions data that schools and policymakers have access to.

- Excluded pupils are more likely to live in poverty and to interact with social services, and are ten times more likely to have recognised mental health needs.

- Excluded pupils were twice as likely to be taught by an unqualified teacher, and twice as likely to have a supply teacher.

- Regional disparities exist too. For example, a pupil excluded from school in the North East is around eight times more likely to attend an AP rated 'Inadequate' by Ofsted.

Research 4

Agenda Alliance (2022)

'Pushed out left out: Girls Speak: Final report'

The 'Girls Speak' project focused on the lives of young women with multiple unmet needs and their experiences of statutory services. The research, based on in-depth interviews with young women aged 13 to 26, shows that when statutory services, and some non-specialist youth services, assumed so-called 'gender-blind' approaches, this led to the specific and gendered needs of young women being underestimated.

Key points

- Young women face distinct risks from young men, and gender-blind policy fails to consider these distinct risks.

- Statutory services are often inaccessible for young women with multiple unmet needs, due to the barriers limiting access. Barriers might include: concerns about being judged or stigmatised by service providers; difficulty in reaching service locations, due to limited transportation options; or services only being available during standard working hours, which may not be accessible to those with conflicting commitments (e.g. young children, multiple jobs or being a young carer).

- Every missed opportunity to help a young woman with multiple unmet needs causes harm and pushes her further away from getting the support she deserves. This can mean that young women are pushed further towards school and social exclusion.

- This can intersect with bias towards other aspects of their identity. For example, dual heritage girls from a mixed White and Black Caribbean background were excluded at three times the rate of their White British counterparts during the years 2019/20 and 2020/21.

Research 5

Centre for Social Justice (2024a, 2024b)

'Suspending Reality'

This recent report explores the growing problem of school exclusions in England, especially how they affect vulnerable young people. It shows that exclusion rates have gone up, partly due to school closures during the pandemic and wider issues in the education system. The research look at how certain accountability rules can encourage schools to exclude more pupils, particularly those with special educational needs or pupils facing disadvantage. They argue for changes to make schools more inclusive and ensure all children get the support they need to succeed.

'Suspending Reality: Part 1' investigates the growing trends in school exclusions and critiques how well the current education system supports vulnerable pupils. It highlights how high accountability measures in education might unintentionally discourage schools from being inclusive.

'Suspending Reality: Part 2' explores the reasons behind the increasing rates of school exclusions, particularly within multi-academy trusts. Drawing insights from discussions with education leaders, it focuses on the difficulties faced by trusts that have taken over struggling schools, which often deal with complex challenges.

Key points

- The research highlights a need for a national inclusion framework for schools and academy trusts. This framework could be used to define inclusion clearly and provide guidance on supporting pupils with additional vulnerabilities, such as those eligible for free school meals, with special educational needs, or who are involved with social services.

- There should be a formal review and better recording systems for managed moves in schools and trusts from government and policy makers. This will help to ensure a rigour and fairness to how these processes are used.

- Multi-academy trusts should collaborate with other trusts and AP sectors to develop local area inclusion strategies. This could be especially beneficial in communities or areas impacted by high levels of socioeconomic disadvantage.

- Multi-academy trusts are encouraged to bid for their own AP and free schools or expand their current capacity, in order to ease the pressure on the sector and improve local provision. This might further support collaboration and information sharing of best practice, particularly around key pupils or vulnerable groups in the community.

Other useful research

- **Baker and Simpson (2020):** This book explore the ways in which schools can address educational inequality through better approaches to behaviour for learning. One recommended approach is for leaders to design behaviour policies and processes that move from a language of 'zero tolerance' towards restorative approaches.

- **Jensen (2009):** This book explores how disciplinary measures in schools and overall school environments can add significant stress, affecting brain function. This unmanaged stress can result in what is known as 'allostatic load'. Instead of returning to a healthy baseline, the developing brain adjusts to negative experiences, becoming either overly reactive or less responsive to stressors. Research into these patterns should be considered when designing and implementing processes for responding to negative behaviours.

Research takeaways

- Research indicates correlations between disadvantage and school exclusions.
- Excluded pupils are more likely to live in poverty, to interact with social services and to have recognised mental health needs.
- Poverty can impact the parental–school relationship and interactions, especially during the formality of exclusion processes.
- Young women face distinct risks from young men, and gender-blind policy fails to consider these distinct risks. For example, statutory services are often inaccessible for young women with multiple unmet needs, due to the barriers limiting access.
- High accountability rules and measures can encourage schools to exclude more pupils, particularly those with special needs or pupils facing disadvantage.

Case study

Horizon School - alternative provision in Hartlepool

Martyn Gordon

During my first year as headteacher of a Pupil Referral Unit (PRU) and Home and Hospital service in Hartlepool, a town that faces high levels of poverty and hardship, I encountered a series of unprecedented challenges due to the COVID-19 pandemic. Despite successfully navigating early hurdles such as Ofsted inspections and financial audits, the pandemic presented a new level of complexity, particularly with staff needing to self-isolate.

We wanted our pupils and local communities to understand that alternative provision is not a lesser form of education and that our pupils have the same potential to achieve as others in mainstream settings. We also wanted to foster in our pupils a commitment to serving their local community, especially in what was a complex and uncharted time for them.

To address the immediate needs of our community, we launched a food bank initiative from our school. We publicised the appeal widely, receiving overwhelming support from local schools, media and residents. Our pupils actively participated in sorting donations into hampers, which we then delivered to vulnerable individuals across town. The initiative gained recognition in the local newspaper, boosting morale and community spirit.

Additionally, our school's newspaper and radio station played a crucial role during the crisis. We extended our media outreach to care homes in collaboration with local social care services, providing residents with uplifting content including a special V.E. Day edition. These projects not only benefited the broader community but also empowered our pupils, fostering intergenerational connections and challenging stereotypes associated with PRU pupils.

Throughout this challenging period, we maintained close partnerships with organisations such as the Children's Hub and local food banks to ensure ongoing support for those in need, even during partial school closures. The generosity of local supermarkets and our continued engagement in project-based learning further enriched our efforts, demonstrating the effectiveness of collaborative networks during times of crisis. Our pupils really benefited from these projects, as they helped break down intergenerational barriers. It was also important to me to challenge some stereotypes of how AP pupils are perceived.

We established four core values in our provision – Consideration, Aspiration, Resilience and Endeavour, combining these to come together as 'CARE'. Our pupils, working closely with their community, were able to show a genuine commitment to CARE in action.

 Ideas to try

Behaviour processes and policies will look different for each individual school. We have provided some practical approaches to consider in tackling poverty-related barriers to school and behaviour.

Proactive versus reactive policies

Baker and Simpson (2020) write about the ways in which disadvantaged pupils are more likely to benefit from non-confrontational approaches to modifying behaviour. Of course, on occasions, children and young people will make mistakes – significantly so in some cases. It is at these points when a school's behaviour policy and processes are tested. Here are some ways to stress-test your processes.

Through the eyes of an ECT

Consider the extent to which behaviour policies make sense and are actionable to an ECT. If they do not make sense to a new starter, then they are unlikely to have the impact that schools want them to have for pupils. Arrange for routine reviews of the policies and their application by ECTs.

In practice, this could involve asking a group of ECTs to review policies or procedures with their mentors or senior leaders. Ask them to summarise how they would do this in practice and to walk each other through the process. You could invite an ECT to work through the reflective tasks at the end of this chapter with other teachers or leaders.

Simulate exclusion

Simulate 'mock' exclusion processes. In practice, this might involve asking a governor and senior leader to structure a mock-style pupil exclusion panel. Invite parents and the pupil to this process. Explain that it is semi-formal and will simulate what would be expected in a formal exclusion process. It is important to inform the pupil and family that this is being used as a preventative measure to help the pupil understand what will follow if behaviour does not improve. It can also help leaders to escalate a response to negative behaviour and be proactive as opposed to wholly reactive. These simulated exclusion processes should be approached with sensitivity, and be framed as supportive and preventative, not punitive. It is essential to clearly communicate to pupils and families that the process is designed to help them understand the implications of continued negative behavior while giving a chance to work collaboratively towards improvement.

Restorative meetings

Create opportunity for restorative meetings with the perpetrators and, if appropriate, with families and victims. This sort of meeting needs to be facilitated carefully but can be useful for helping pupils understand the impact of persistent bad choices in the community. For example, you could ask pupils/colleagues to comment on how the behaviour impacted them, how it has negatively impacted learning or what might be needed to further repair or restore the relationship.

In one memorable example, a caretaker explained how physical damage of school toilets was creating him additional workload and stress. The pupil simply hadn't considered this and agreed to do some work experience with the caretaker after school in place of several detentions. The result was that the pupil never vandalised school property again.

Look at language

Ask how much leaders understand policies and procedures around the school exclusion policy and how accessible this is to disadvantaged families. This is particularly important where English is spoken as an additional language or where there are perceived or known learning difficulties in families. Consider the terminology and language that is used in formal communication to families. It can be helpful to ask a SENDCo to proofread and help to ensure that the wording is accessible and that parents will be able to make sense of it.

Balance expectations with empathy

High expectations are an important part of raising standards. These need to be balanced with an understanding of the needs of pupils and poverty-related barriers to learning.

Practical approaches to this might include the following:

Friday praise

Ask teachers to commit to regularly giving praise at the end of a school week. Identify an example of positive behaviour or achievement. Refer to Chapter 12 to understand how mentoring could be used to facilitate this.

Accessible progress meetings

Make sure that academic progress meetings are at a time suitable for disadvantaged families. Consider the timing, location and logistics of these meetings carefully to ensure that low-income families are able to attend. Sometimes schools use a language of 'hard to reach' parents but, in some cases, schools might be hard for parents to engage with.

Understanding individual needs

Many schools start each academic term by giving teachers an overview of key pupils and their needs. It is important to make sure that this is conveyed sensitively and in a way that provides teachers and staff with ideas on how to respond to need. Understanding cognitive science and memory can improve how we plan staff training and meetings focused on behaviour. For instance, having behaviour leaders regularly share information is more effective than occasional events. It may also be helpful to ensure that staff have the opportunity to consider what has been shared and act on this in their lesson and curriculum planning time (e.g. planning for specific behaviour or barriers to learning that will surface as a result of the need).

No silos

Local behaviour and attendance partnerships can help schools to have an overview of families and pupil need and challenge, and help professionals with the interventions they have in place to support pupils. Examples might include attendance research hubs, collaboration between local authorities, clusters of schools and multi-academy trusts.

Alternative provision specialists

Sometimes mainstream teachers and leaders might have a misconception that AP does not equate to good education. Invite AP specialists to share their curriculum pathways. This can be a useful way of ensuring schools understand what opportunities exist to help support pupils facing disadvantage or poverty-related barriers to learning.

Outreach

Explore how AP teachers could work alongside teachers in mainstream settings to support in managing complex behaviour. For example, an AP teacher could observe classroom behaviours and provide the teacher with some specific strategies to tackle particular types of behaviours. You could also ask AP teachers to look at your behaviour policy and consider how well this is implemented, during a learning walk alongside leaders and teachers.

'What works' case studies

Provide opportunity for case studies to be shared of pupils where there has been a reduction in exclusions. This can be helpful for understanding and sharing intelligence on what is working locally and around specific types of behaviours. This does not need to be overly detailed or burdensome with excessive documentation. The case study should briefly outline the barriers the pupil has encountered, describe the interventions implemented and highlight the resulting impact on attendance and engagement in lessons (such as behaviour data). Including comments from the pupil or staff member can add additional insight and depth to these case studies.

Closing gaps in classrooms

Pupils routinely facing exclusion are at risk of gaps appearing in their learning. Whilst schools are legally bound to ensure that educational provision is maintained during periods of exclusion, the reality is that some pupils will not engage with it. The following approaches can be helpful in supporting pupils' transition back into school after a period of exclusion.

Sorry we missed you

Include a 'sorry we missed you' sheet in pupil work. It can highlight important knowledge that might have been missed during the period of absence or exclusion. Keep the note positive, with a clear focus on what the pupil can do to catch up on one or two aspects of missed learning. See the example template below.

Sorry we missed you!
Hi (name of pupil). It is great having you back in the lesson. Recently you missed out on these important topics/lessons in (name of subject). [The teacher should write one to three key topics here]
To help support your learning, focus on this target… [Teacher writes a specific target or task that the pupil should do]
These could be pre-printed and highlighted based on which is most important for the pupil.

Reintegrating into lessons

Identify the subjects in which pupils have some record of success and where pre-existing positive relationships exist with teachers. This could then be used in a reintegration meeting with the pupil and parent. For example, a pastoral leader could share comments from teachers with the pupil and parent/carer, or subject data that shows where behaviour has shown improvement or progress. This can be especially useful if leaders are trying to help pupils and parents/carers understand that aspects of the behaviour are chosen and deliberate. For pupils then reintegrating on a flexible timetable (e.g. some attendance in formal lessons, some time with pastoral support staff), prioritise the lessons where the pupil has a proven track record of some success.

Community curriculum

Provide opportunities for pupils to get behind a cause that matters to them. This can support pupils in understanding their civic responsibility and gaining a greater sense of belonging to the school. Examples might include supporting a charity endeavour, such as a Christmas shoebox appeal in which pupils ask for donations and make up a shoebox of gifts that is sent to a local charity to distribute.

The Difference – specialist leadership development

The Difference is a charity dedicated to developing specialist school leaders capable of tackling social exclusion within schools. Their objective is to enhance outcomes for vulnerable pupils through tailored leadership training and interventions. The Difference aims to equip school leaders with the skills and knowledge required to establish inclusive environments that cater to the needs of all pupils, particularly those at risk of exclusion. You can find out more about the work of The Difference and their support opportunities in the links at the end of the chapter.

Chapter takeaways

- School behaviour and exclusion policies and processes need to be proactive rather than reactive.
- It is important for leaders to evaluate the ways in which these processes are understood by all adults. Check the extent to which they are understood by new employees and ECTs.
- Language used in exclusion processes needs to be understood by all stakeholders. Ensure support is provided that helps disadvantaged families and pupils to understand it.
- Hyperlocal intelligence is needed when it comes to understanding the needs of pupils and sense-checking what is likely to make a difference.
- Partnership across multiple agencies and education settings is invaluable.

Recap and Reflective tasks

Recap

Indicate which statements are true or false based on your understanding.	True	False
Unofficial methods of exclusion in the UK obscure the true extent of exclusionary practices, particularly their impact on pupils facing poverty and disadvantage.		
Significant research demonstrates that excluded pupils are more likely to live in poverty and to interact with social services.		
Some research indicates that low-income families had feelings of ineffectiveness and feeling solely responsible for all aspects of the challenges faced by their child when faced with formal and informal exclusion processes.		

Reflective tasks

Reflective task for leaders and teacher educators
• Review the school(s) behaviour policies with a recently recruited member of staff and/or an ECT. • Make a note of key terms and phrases that are used to demonstrate the values and ethos of your school(s).

Sit with a group of other leaders and/or teacher educators in your school(s). Invite them to each complete the above activity. Then consider and summarise:

According to leaders:	According to ECTs/newly appointed staff:
What are the core values and principles that underpin our approach to promoting positive behaviour as a whole school?	What are the core values and principles that underpin our approach to promoting positive behaviour as a whole school?

What, then, is our shared and coherent understanding of what this looks like in practice:

in classrooms?

in corridors?

as part of our approach to managing exclusions and persistently disruptive behaviour?

Focus on a key pupil/family

For this activity, focus on a specific pupil who is at risk of persistent or permanent exclusion, along with their family environment. For the purposes of confidentiality and integrity, you may wish to consider initials or anonymising content for note-keeping.

Reactive:	Proactive:
What reactive measures have been put in place as a result of disruptive behaviour incidents from this pupil?	What proactive measures have been put in place as a result of disruptive behaviour incidents from this pupil?

Consider a simulated or actual exclusion process for this pupil and the experience of their family. What barriers to understanding may need to be considered and how?

Language used in the process:
(You may wish to refer to the glossary on page 271 as part of this.)

Communications issued to the pupil/their family:
(Examples: letter, information pack, teacher-set work.)

Logistics and mechanics of the meeting(s):
(Examples: location, timing, formality, informal processes.)

Follow-up:
(Examples: checking parent/carer understanding of the outputs and next steps.)

Feedback
(Examples: how might you ensure feedback is collected based on the experience of the pupil and their family, and used to inform future meetings with this or other pupils?)

Reflective task for teachers/curriculum leaders

- Having read this chapter, what are the main implications for you as a classroom teacher and/or curriculum leader?

Breaking the cycle of exclusion through classroom and curriculum practice
These reflections are designed to consider how you can contribute to breaking the cycle of school and social exclusion as a classroom teacher and/or curriculum leader. These are important as part of a holistic whole-school approach to responding to the needs of vulnerable pupils.

Imagine a pupil is soon to be reintegrated following an FTE or period of absence. Identify one aspect of your current curriculum/programme that this pupil might struggle to understand.

What are some of the ways in which you can support their reintegration back into the curriculum/classroom in light of this?	
Catch-up curriculum activities and tasks designed to help their knowledge:	Individual pupil support strategies to respond to and promote positive behaviour/conduct:

Consider how you can learn more about the needs of the pupil and share your own classroom/curriculum intelligence about how the pupil is managing.	
Where can I find additional information about the specific needs and known barriers to learning?	How can I share additional feedback about this pupil's ongoing work in my classroom/curriculum areas and with whom?

Based on your reading in this chapter, consider the specific ways in which you can further develop your own expertise about school and social exclusion in your career as an educator.	
Ways in which I can further understand the reality of poverty and its link to exclusion in my own school(s) or team(s):	Ways in which I can further develop my own expertise of this agenda as a classroom teacher or curriculum leader in my career pathway:

📖 Further reading

Harris and Gordon (2022) – 'Breaking the cycle of poverty and exclusion'
Paget et al. (2018) – 'Which children and young people are excluded from school? Findings from a large British birth cohort study, the Avon Longitudinal Study of Parents and Children (ALSPAC)'
Simpson (2023) – 'Canary in the mine: what white working-class underachievement reveals about processes of marginalisation in English secondary education'
Toth et al. (2023) – 'From a child who IS a problem to a child who HAS a problem: Fixed period school exclusions and mental health outcomes from routine outcome monitoring among children and young people attending school counselling'

Links

The Difference: www.the-difference.com
The Centre for Social Justice: www.centreforsocialjustice.org.uk

11 Partnerships
John Smith

Chapter summary

Schools can build partnerships with other organisations to better understand and tackle poverty at scale. In this chapter, we explore some of the key principles involved in building effective partnerships in schools.

 What does the research suggest?

In this section, we explore some of the research and literature that has supported our teams and other schools in developing partnership collaboration as a means of tackling poverty and disadvantage in schools.

Research 1

School Partnerships Alliance (2022)

'School partnerships for impact guide: Laying the groundwork for enabling and promoting meaningful partnerships between different schools across the state and independent sectors'

This report was commissioned by the School Partnerships Alliance, which supports partnerships between the independent and state sectors. The foundational question investigated is: how can schools improve through partnerships between schools and with external agencies?

Key points

A summary of the report includes:

- There is value in understanding 'collaborative advantage' – the idea that we can amplify and multiply individual contributions by pooling resources towards a common goal. This term is well understood in industry, but under used in education.

- Well-planned and strategic partnership projects can bring demonstrable benefits to all participating partners. When local schools, charities and other organisations put their collective skills, resources and funds towards a shared endeavour, they can become more than the sum of their parts.
- The report provides examples of where this can work in schools and other organisations, including projects, from small beginnings and pilots to more formal partnerships.

Research 2

Ainscow et al. (2023)

'Turning the tide: A study of place-based school partnerships'

This study provides an evidence-based analysis of eight regional multi-school partnerships. The findings are presented in relation to the broader question of whether opening education to market forces in the UK (e.g. academisation, free schools) has had a positive impact on school improvement.

The evidence suggests that, at a system level, this approach may have negatively impacted communities and children who experience disadvantage. In this context, 'system level' can refer to the education system as a whole, rather than individual schools or localised contexts. It implies looking at the collective effects of policies and processes, e.g. a collaboration of schools and cross sector organisations could work together to tackle particular nuanced issues specific to that context. However, the study also highlights the value of hyperlocal partnerships in helping to tackle facets of poverty and disadvantage in communities.

Key points

The research indicates that hyperlocal partnerships should be:

- led locally by credible and experienced school leaders
- underpinned with a clear purpose and intent
- evidence-based when making decisions
- aware of the specific local barriers and context
- inclusive and linked to wider community resources (e.g. local funding streams or charitable resources).

Research 3

Fiennes (2012)

It Ain't What You Give, It's the Way That You Give It: Making Charitable Donations That Get Results

This book explains the work of the charity sector, so that donors can be empowered to make more informed decisions when deciding who and what to donate to. The book includes many concepts that may be unfamiliar to school leaders and teachers who haven't worked in the charity sector. The main themes are unpacked further in this chapter, and several key ideas have important implications for helping to tackle poverty and disadvantage by way of fundraising in schools.

Key points

- Fiennes unpacks the idea of 'funding amplifiers', one of the most misunderstood aspects of the charity sector. This is the idea that charities can multiply or 'amplify' the value of initial funds/donations in kind.

- We can understand the concept of 'funding amplification' when contrasted with 'funding depletion': donors may fear that their donation is depleted on its way through the machinery of a charity. However, the research shows that the best charities actually add value to the original donation; these are funding amplifiers.

- The positive impact of admin resource can be overlooked: whilst a donor may feel that they want their funding to go directly to the beneficiary (without being 'depleted' on the way via admin costs or similar), often it is through the admin function that a charity can amplify the initial funds – for example, by exploring bulk discounts or processing Gift Aid.

Research takeaways

- Schools can make their resources go further by partnering with other schools and organisations towards a common goal.
- There are a range of partnership models, from loose alliances for small projects through to more formal alliances across an area or place.

- Schools can make external funding go further by adding value and learning from other industries and sectors (e.g. charities).
- There may be activities and approaches that work in one locality or context but which may not be appropriate in others. Decision-making needs to occur at a local level in order to address place-specific problems.

 Case Study

Theory of Change: Starting with the end in mind

In brief, Theory of Change (ToC) is an approach that works backwards from a well-articulated long-term objective through the steps needed to achieve it.

Step 1: What do we want to achieve?

- Leaders need to define where the steps are leading. Collins (2001) calls this 'the Big Hairy Audacious Goal (BHAG)'. Leaders do not take direct responsibility for the entirety of the BHAG. However, it is important for leaders to be aware of the aspects of the BHAG that they can impact. This is the key difference between impact and outcomes.
- For example, DePaul UK is a charity tackling homelessness and supporting vulnerable young people. Various schools across the country work in partnership with this charity. The BHAG for DePaul UK is *to end homelessness for all young people*. In a Theory of Change, this long-term objective can be placed above an 'accountability ceiling', meaning that DePaul is not solely accountable for this Big Hairy Audacious Goal, but can put steps in place to help work towards it in partnership with schools and other organisations.

Step 2: How will we achieve it?

- The 'outcomes' level of a ToC should be constructed so that the causal links to the long-term goal are clear and concrete.
- Leaders do not need to do the research to prove the causality; that can arguably be found through other sources (perhaps even in this book!).
- The ToC is a call to action based on robust research. It can be useful for helping to summarise to other colleagues in schools and organisations what is needed and a framework for how this might be achieved.

Step 3: How will we know we have been successful?

- Fiennes (2012) introduces the idea of 'breadth versus certainty'.
- Leaders can think of interventions as lying on a sliding scale from 'broad and shallow' to 'narrow and deep'.
- This can be visualised by a triangle, where interventions around an individual or small group, which are easier to track and more likely to succeed (narrow and deep), are positioned at the top. However, those interventions nearer the base aim at a broader scope but are more difficult to attribute impact (broad and shallow).

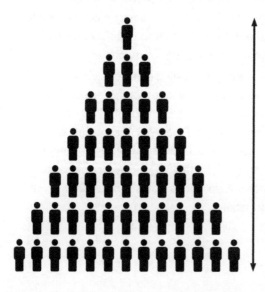

Narrow and Deep
= high certainty of impact; low reach

Broad and Shallow
= low certainty of impact; high reach

In the case of independent schools, giving fundings to a bursary or scholarship would sit at the point of the triangle. Bursaries offer depth of experience for individuals and impact is easier to track. Conversely, partnership and outreach activities can affect many more pupils but it can be more difficult to attribute impact. Think of a careers event for primary-age pupils: schools can plant the 'golden seeds' and aim to change attitudes and norms, but charting a long-term and lasting impact is complex for teachers and industry advocates. Schools might need to tailor Key Performance Indicators (KPIs), depending on where activities sit on the triangle.

In our community and outreach work, our school settled on a model that links with the triangle:

- Where the intervention is less certain or measurable, leaders and teachers aim to reach big numbers of pupils, usually at primary age.
- Whilst the impact is hard to measure and to attribute over time, planting as many seeds as possible increases the likelihood that some may flower, especially when aiming to raise aspirations and cultural capital.
- This is where leaders and teachers might collect quantitative 'output' data, such as number of attendees or feedback scales. All of this can help to tell the story of impact for these pupils.
- At the top of the triangle, more targeted interventions for smaller groups of individuals are much easier to attribute impact, and therefore justify the relative time and cost resources (e.g. supporting with the writing of an application to university or one-to-one tutoring).
- This is where leaders and teachers might use pupil outcome data in exams or in-class assessment.

Multiplier effects in fundraising

In our partnership work amongst schools and charities in the North East, the school benefits from generous funding from foundations, businesses and philanthropists. This will not be a reality for all schools. However, a challenge for our school is how to make these funds go as far as possible, because we cannot rely on limitless funding, especially in economically uncertain times.

In the next section, there are some examples of multiplier effects that school leaders and teachers might find useful in putting together more robust funding bids. The key is to focus not only on what schools will do with the funds, but also on how leaders and the whole school can add value to the funds.

 Ideas to try

In this section, I have summarised some of the tools and methods that have supported other school leaders, teachers and me in growing partnerships. The reflective tasks at the end of the chapter are designed to help colleagues grow in their understanding of the tools and approaches to this.

Grow a volunteer army

Many charities rely heavily on volunteers. When funders donate to a charity with a strong volunteer base, they are drawing on a volunteer army to work towards their chosen cause, to which they would otherwise have no access.

In partnership work between schools, leaders and teachers might do this through pupil volunteering.

Example

Voluntary Service Readers reach hundreds of primary-age children on a weekly basis in our school, using their phonics training to enhance reading progress. Furthermore, these pupils provide positive role models and the volunteers themselves gain a great deal.

Develop local expertise and external collaboration

One of the main benefits of giving to charities is of course their forensic knowledge of the problem that they exist to address, whether that be through direct relationships with the beneficiaries or through the cumulative know-how of their organisations and networks.

In my role, I have benefited greatly from the time and knowledge of my colleagues and peers, both locally and nationally, in growing partnership work. Consider the problems that exist locally and which matter to your school context. Then identify the local networks, collaborations and champions that care about addressing these topics. This is much harder to do if your school has not defined or identified the problem that they want to address.

Produce a proof of concept

School leaders must be able to articulate where they are on a journey with each project through school development plans.

It may be that a pioneering funder would like to give to experimental pilots exploring the 'art of the possible', but (more likely) funders will need to see 'proof of concept' before getting involved. This depends on the quality of impact evaluation.

It is important for leaders in schools to understand that funders are more likely to give to a project when they see evidence of a pilot implementation or a tested product being further scaled. Therefore, leaders and teachers should have strategic school documentation in place to support this.

Create ripple effects

There are causes that might be better served by system-level impact. For example, changes in educational policy at a national level can have a deep impact across millions of children and families, which even the best of projects cannot always achieve, even with focused funding.

Understand economies of scale

A good procurement officer can make smart decisions around purchases that just can't be leveraged at a smaller scale.

The administration of Gift Aid and other direct financial benefits can be significant – this is perhaps the most obvious way that charities can multiply funding from the outset. It is likely that many school leaders and teachers will have limited experience of this. Therefore, consider where additional finance training might be needed.

Schools might also benefit by making deliberate appointments to trustee or governance boards of personnel who have experience of these areas from other sectors.

Consider infrastructure

When donating through a school or a larger charity, the infrastructure of the organisation can cover many of the smaller (but essential) mechanics that make activities happen. These smaller activities can accumulate to facilitate ambitious projects. For example, office space, administrative support, photocopying, technology support, stationery – these all need to be considered when applying for funding and producing prospective budgets for grant use.

Sometimes school leaders and teachers might overlook these needs. This reinforces the need for schools to work in collaboration with others who have experience of this and who can be a critical friend when assessing the quality of a funding application.

Impact and evaluation

Robust impact evaluation is fundamental to getting value for money and to creating that virtuous circle of confidence in the whole endeavour: creating momentum by demonstrating and telling the story of past success.

As one trustee of a foundation told me recently, when asking for a certain format of impact-reporting, 'We want to know what we bought for our money and how you know.'

Not all funders will be as direct, but they probably should be – charitable funds are not limitless amidst recent economic turbulence. If schools and charities cannot show results, funding may well go to another organisation who can demonstrate this more effectively. Therefore, make sure that sufficient time, capacity and expertise are deployed towards helping school leaders and teachers evaluate impact.

Schools might benefit from collaborating with charities and third-sector organisations to help them achieve this beyond the orthodox school approaches of measuring impact purely through pupil outcome data.

Embrace technology

Where technology can be harnessed well, efficiencies can often follow. For example, the evolution of virtual CPD, conferences and meetings has arguably reduced the amount of travel time that school leaders and teachers once undertook.

Consider the extent to which technology and software are used robustly to grow partnerships.

Social media and virtual platforms can also be a useful way of demonstrating to funders and prospective funders that money is being used to grow the impact of the school in the community.

Consider administration costs

It is important for schools to consider and budget for the additional administrative costs that might exist because of innovation and new projects being funded. This should also form part of a clear and logical implementation plan.

Chapter takeaways

- Theory of Change (ToC) is a backward-looking approach from long-term objectives to steps needed to achieve them. This can support school leaders in helping to implement specific projects aimed at tackling poverty and disadvantage in schools.
- School leaders and teachers can use the ToC to identify specific goals that they want to address, create clear causal links to a long-term objective and determine measurable outcomes to assess success.
- Multiplier effects in fundraising can include leveraging volunteer support, local expertise and developing a proof of concept. This can be further achieved through impactful evaluation of projects and ensuring that the project outcomes are communicated well to stakeholders.
- Effective fundraising strategies involve demonstrating value for money, utilising technology for efficiency and budgeting for administrative costs to maximise impact. Schools are well-placed to achieve this, but it requires a clear implementation plan.

⊞ Recap and Reflective tasks

Recap

Indicate which statements are true or false based on your understanding.	True	False
Theory of Change requires teachers and school leaders to carry out their own action research.		
The Theory of Change methodology helps school leaders and teachers articulate clear goals, establish causal relationships between interventions and outcomes, and measure success effectively.		
Schools embarking on innovative projects typically do not need to consider or budget for additional administrative costs, as such projects are usually self-sustaining once implemented.		
In educational charitable giving, it is more impactful to give funds directly to the beneficiary.		
All KPIs should be quantitative so we can analyse the data.		

Reflective tasks

Reflective task for leaders and teachers
These are suitable for leaders/teachers working in collaboration with others on a specific project. You may find this helpful to do as part of a group exercise with colleagues.
Working backwards: • In one sentence, can you articulate the long-term objective of the project?

- Next, write three to four outcomes that have solid causal links to the long-term objective.
  Remember, the idea is that this is based on existing research (some of which is in this book!).

- Activities and KPIs: What are the activities that will make these outcomes happen?
- How will you/colleagues know whether they have been successful?

Theory of change template
Examples are widely available online. Here is an example of a template to support discussion with colleagues.

Long-term objective ('Big Hairy Audacious Goal'):

Outcome
Example: More pupils take maths post-16 (must have causal link to long-term objective)

Activities
Example: Further maths GCSE webinars for pupils

KPIs
Example:
- Percentage of pupils achieving level 4+ in maths
- Numbers taking part year on year

Resources needed
Example:
- Funded teaching hours
- Exam entry administration support
- Travel to in-person events

Reflective task for leaders and teachers following the previous activity	
Once you have produced your ToC, share it with stakeholders to see whether it makes sense to others. Examples of stakeholders might include: • Teachers sharing this as part of a senior leadership meeting. • Senior leaders sharing this as part of a governor/trustee meeting.	
Is the Theory of Change...	Reflections based on feedback
...plausible? • Is there a causal link from each outcome to the long-term objective? • How robust is the evidence behind this assumed causal link?	
...feasible? • What resource is needed to achieve the activities? • Do we have access to the resource needed? • Is the timeframe 'doable'? Has this been broken down appropriately?	
...testable? • Are the KPIs measurable and understood? • How can we tell if the outcomes have been achieved?	
Conclusion: • What do we need to adapt about our ToC in order to ensure it is understood? • What additional implementation considerations are needed? • When will we revisit the ToC and project(s) with stakeholders?	

 Further reading

Taplin et al. (2013) – 'Theory of change technical papers: A series of papers to support development of theories of change based on practice in the field'.

Links

DePaul youth homelessness charity: www.depaul.org.uk

Giving Evidence: giving-evidence.com

NCVO – Theory of Change: www.ncvo.org.uk/help-and-guidance/strategy-and-impact/strategy-and-business-planning/theory-of-change

RGS Newcastle – Partnerships – Social impact review: https://issuu.com/rgsnewcastle/docs/rgs_impactreport_web_version_final

12 Mentoring

David Linsell

Chapter summary

The Kemnal Academies Trust (TKAT) is a multi-academy trust with 45 primary, secondary and special schools across the south and east regions of England. Many of these schools serve areas of disadvantage, and the overall pupil premium rate is close to 40 per cent.

During school closures at the height of the COVID-19 pandemic, pastoral staff made welfare phone calls to vulnerable families on a regular basis. These were different to how TKAT schools had carried out the calls before, because they were not problem-focused and led to pupils seemingly opening up about everyday experiences. The TKAT ACE programme was created from this, with a focus on establishing 'A Champion for Every Child' (ACE). It has had a measurable impact for thousands of pupil premium pupils across TKAT.

In this chapter, we share how ACE has been further developed across TKAT schools and its impact on helping to tackle poverty-related barriers to learning and disadvantage.

 What does the research suggest?

TKAT ACE developed from pastoral staff engaging with pupils and families regularly. However, TKAT has used the following research insights to help strengthen ACE and the work of ACE tutors. This research has been particularly helpful for staff at TKAT in understanding how to implement and evaluate the processes that have been put in place to support pupils facing disadvantage and poverty-related barriers to learning.

Research 1

EEF (2024)

'A school's guide to implementation'

Effective implementation was key to ensuring that the TKAT ACE programme could have an impact for pupils. The EEF (2019) 'Putting evidence to work' guidance report was an important part of this. Since the development of TKAT ACE, a more up-to-date guidance report has been published by the EEF (2024): 'A school's guide to implementation'.

The guidance report aims to help schools use evidence-based approaches to improve effective implementation of teaching and learning strategies in schools. The report provides three strategic recommendations to help schools give ideas and innovations the best chance of success by considering carefully how to effectively introduce, implement and monitor the impact of an intervention.

Key points

- **Adopt the behaviours that drive effective implementation:** Effective implementation involves engaging stakeholders in shaping outcomes, uniting them around the initiative's implementation, and reflecting, monitoring and adapting to enhance ongoing improvement.

- **Attend to the contextual factors that influence implementation:** Work to ensure that implementation is evidence-informed, appropriate for the context and feasible, whilst developing supportive systems and structures such as time allocation and data systems, and ensuring that change can be supported.

- **Use a structured but flexible implementation process:** Use a structured approach to integrate behaviours and contextual factors into your daily tasks, utilising a practical and customised set of implementation strategies, organised into manageable phases.

An important insight gained by colleagues engaged in developing TKAT ACE, alongside research guidance from the EEF, was the recognition that implementation should be viewed and treated as an ongoing process of learning and enhancement.

Research 2

TKAT: Pilot research

Learning from small-scale implementation

Our second important implementation decision was to use small-scale pilot projects of ACE so that we could learn from pupils about the programme and adapt it accordingly. TKAT started the ACE programme in September 2020 with a pilot in seven schools ranging from primary to secondary and including special school provision. The pilot research projects became integral to the success of the programme because leaders needed to learn what worked in their own school context. Schools benefited from understanding that this was a long-term project because building relationships takes time.

Key points

Key findings from the small-scale research included:

- There was a significant benefit to schools being able to collaborate to share their insights and best-practice approaches with each other.
- PP pupils appreciated having a regular one-to-one opportunity to meet with their ACE tutor.
- The ACE tutor would regularly identify issues and barriers to learning by having a routine call with families that otherwise might have been missed or misunderstood.

Following the success of a small-scale pilot, all 45 TKAT schools implemented their own pilot projects in September 2021. This led to TKAT appointing Regional Leads (RLs). These are school-based ACE leaders given time to support other schools in their area. The brief was to provide support and challenge to their schools, sharing expertise and holding schools to account for implementation. In 2022, TKAT moved to a full implementation of the programme, with the aim of all 8,500 PP pupils in TKAT schools benefiting from an ACE tutor.

Research 3

ImpactEd (2022)

ACE evaluation summary

TKAT was keen to ensure that ACE could be evaluated promptly so that leaders would be able to understand what was working and how to improve the programme for pupils. With this in mind, ImpactEd were used to carry out an evaluation of the programme. This included working with leaders, teachers, pupils and assessment data to understand more about the impact of ACE.

ImpactEd (2022) published an evaluation of the ACE programme, based on four distinct research questions which were co-constructed with TKAT leaders:

- What is the impact of ACE on academic attainment on those who took part?
- What is the impact of ACE on skills relating to engagement and behaviour, including goal orientation, school engagement, self-efficacy and motivation?
- How do these social and emotional skills vary for pupil premium pupils who took part in ACE compared to the PP national averages?
- What factors underpin successful implementation of ACE?

The evaluation research report concludes that ACE is having an effective impact in TKAT schools, particularly in relation to supporting disadvantaged pupils in overcoming poverty-related barriers to learning. In particular, the report highlights that ACE is leading to an increase in pupil attainment in maths and on levels of pupil motivation.

Key points

A high-level summary of the findings from the evaluation include:

- Outcomes in maths improved in all participating primary schools, and reading in all except one. This was despite some of the schools being disrupted by partial closures during the pandemic.
- Statistically significant improvements were seen in pupils' self-reported levels of goal orientation, self-efficacy and motivation. Improvements were also seen in reported levels of school engagement. This was also supported by ACE tutor observations and insights.
- Qualitative data indicated that key success factors for the programme were the availability of support networks for tutors, the quality of training and its personalised and one-to-one nature.
- The quality of teacher/tutor communication was highlighted as a key area to continue to prioritise in order to sustain and further develop the impact of the programme in other settings.

Case Study

Gray's Farm Primary Academy – ACE

In this case study, we provide an example of how one school has put into practice the TKAT ACE programme to support pupils facing disadvantage and poverty-related barriers to learning.

Gray's Farm Primary Academy, located in Kent, serves a student population of 424, with 141 identified as pupil premium beneficiaries. Central to their approach is the TKAT ACE programme, which ensures that all pupil premium pupils have access to dedicated ACE tutors. The frequency of this support is determined by a Red, Amber, Green (RAG) rating system, which assesses individual pastoral needs, social behaviours and attendance records.

Pupils categorised as Red, including those with child protection plans or social services, receive weekly one-to-one sessions with their ACE tutor, supplemented by additional check-ins during breaks or lessons. Those categorised as Amber are seen every two weeks, engaging in both individual and group activities, whilst Green-category pupils have sessions every three weeks, balancing one-to-one interactions with group work.

Parental engagement plays a pivotal role at Gray's Farm, facilitated through active face-to-face contact at the school gate. Parents are encouraged to

Mentoring

approach their child's ACE tutor for updates on home life, fostering a collaborative environment that supports the student's holistic development.

Under the ACE programme, Gray's Farm has successfully initiated various projects aimed at enriching student experiences and fostering community cohesion. These include ACE open mornings, when parents engage with ACE tutors to learn about ongoing initiatives; a LEGO® building competition focused on sustainable community design, with winning entries shared in school assemblies; gardening activities catering to pupils without access to gardens at home; coffee mornings to enhance school–community relationships; a pre-loved uniform swap to support families financially; and dedicated efforts to track and support pupils with attendance issues, ensuring proactive communication with parents regarding tardiness or absences. Through these initiatives, Gray's Farm Primary Academy demonstrates a holistic approach to supporting pupil premium pupils and enhancing overall school culture through the TKAT ACE programme.

Creating a deeper connection with a pupil is founded on personalised attention and individual goal-setting. Through ACE mentoring, school leaders and teachers learned that pupil's self-efficacy and goal-setting were rarely linked to a culture of low aspirations. Pupils did not lack aspirations but often lacked the social capital to be able to articulate these goals. In some cases, pupils believed that they were not capable of achieving what they aspired to become or held the misconception that 'jobs like that are not for young people like me'. Over time, ACE mentors have helped pupils convert their aspiration into something tangible. This is achieved by agreeing on short-term goals related to a pupil's long-term ambition. This approach has been effective with both primary- and secondary-aged pupils, with a focus on what the pupil wants to be rather than simply the job that they want to do.

Here are two examples of pupils who were helped by their ACE mentor, covering the initial issue, the communications involved and the practical ways in which the pupils were helped.

Example A: Year 3 pupil

A Year 3 pupil was withdrawn, not engaged in class and often missed school. The ACE mentor worked with the pupil to understand the underlying causes. The pupil felt that they did not have many friends and found a lot of school boring. They did like football but did not attend the after-school club.

Response: The mentor set them a challenge to persuade one of their few friends to go to after-school football with them, agreed with the parent that their child could attend, made sure the football coach invited them and welcomed them, talked about the football club at a tutor session and praised the pupil in front of their parents.

Example B: Year 10 pupil

A Year 10 pupil was underachieving, particularly in English, and quite often involved in low-level disruption. The ACE mentor found out that they had an interest in becoming a teacher, but did not believe they were clever enough.

Response: The ACE mentor arranged a careers interview to help the pupil understand which qualifications they would need. The ACE mentor spoke to the English teacher, who made some suggestions about wider reading and offered to set some extra work to help with specific English skills. The ACE mentor converted the advice of the English teacher into specific goals, which were shared with the pupil's family.

 Ideas to try

The ACE programme has been carefully designed and implemented over a number of years. However, there are a number of actions which can support schools in further understanding and applying the approach in similar contexts.

Establish your mentoring team

ACE mentors are typically drawn from the teaching assistant or pastoral support workforce. Some schools do use teachers, but this has depended on the levels of pupil need and capacity within the teaching workforce.

Tutor training

TKAT organised internal mandatory training, and all prospective ACE mentors completed this prior to starting in their role. We suggest your training:

- provides enhanced safeguarding
- develops communications skills
- details how to access the resources that support the programme.

In addition, we recommend tutors are given joint supervision sessions to share concerns and learn from each other.

Getting started with your pupils

ACE mentors meet with their pupils for brief sessions of 20 minutes twice a week. The initial focus is 'agenda-free', building a positive relationship with the pupil by talking about what the pupils have achieved and what they (and their families) want to achieve in the future.

Once trust is developing, the tutors aim to diagnose a pupil's barriers to learning. It is important that this is concerned with what matters to the pupils rather than simply based on an overarching school priority or agenda.

Diagnose pupils' barriers to learning

ACE mentors use Maslow's hierarchy of needs to frame this diagnostic conversation. This hierarchy is explored in greater depth in Chapter 4. It is important to note that these themes (e.g. psychological safety, physiological needs) are not ticked off as a set list in order, but simply form a starting point; the actual conversation is based on the pupil's needs.

The aim of the diagnostic session is to end by agreeing goals relating to the pupil's barriers. Goals are then shared with parents if appropriate and reviewed in future meetings.

The conversation with pupils follows several broad lines of enquiry.

- **Physical wellbeing:** Are the pupil's physical needs being cared for? (E.g. food, clothing.)
- **Mental and emotional wellbeing:** Does the pupil feel safe and cared for?
- **Social wellbeing:** Does the pupil have someone to turn to for help?
- **Personal wellbeing**: What goals or ambitions does the pupil have?

Mentors record the pupil's goals and challenges and share this information with the pastoral team and the pupil's teacher(s).

The mentor takes on the role of being the champion for the pupil to ensure they get the support they need to both face barriers and achieve their goals.

Active ingredients

'Active ingredient' is a term adopted by the EEF (2024) to identify key behaviours and content that make a particular intervention or strategy work. Since the inception of the ACE pilot projects, TKAT has designed and outlined the active ingredients of ACE. When using the term 'active ingredients', we have used this to describe the specific actions, principles and practices a school aims to implement through an intervention. This involves clearly identifying the exact goals the approach is designed to achieve. Schools can use these to help inform their own design and delivery of mentoring. We would stress the importance of ensuring schools make careful use of the implementation guidance report and corresponding tools provided freely by the EEF to help inform their implementation plan.

TKAT ACE® — A Champion for Every Child — THE ACTIVE INGREDIENTS

Building relationships
- One-to-one
- Empowering pupils
- Parent partnership

- Accreditation
- Supervision
- Career progression

Championing pupils
- Tackling barriers
- Attendance
- Wider opportunities

- Social Media
- Record keeping
- Communication

Continuing Professional Development

Robust evaluation

The positive relationship that must exist between the tutor and the pupil sits at the core.

Build a positive mentor–pupil relationship

Since the development of the programme, TKAT has identified the following qualities as being important aspects of developing this positive relationship.

- **Genuine authenticity:** ensuring sincerity in the meetings and a commitment to pupils.

- **Active listening:** working hard at picking up on verbal and non-verbal prompts.

Mentoring

- **Empathy and understanding:** demonstrating compassion and showing care.
- **Building trust:** being reliable and following through with actions agreed in meetings.
- **Investment:** investing time and effort, ensuring that the relationship is prioritised.
- **Respecting boundaries:** being mindful of when pupils may not want to discuss challenges.
- **Patience:** being prepared to take time to get to the root of issues and barriers.

One-to-one mentoring

TKAT has trialled the use of small-group ACE mentoring opportunities in an effort to reach more pupils over time. However, these did not have the same meaningful impact as one-to-one mentoring. The qualities and approaches described in the previous paragraph are most effective when the relationship is one-to-one, as the connection with the pupil is founded on personalised attention and goal-setting.

Partnership with parents and carers

Forging positive relationships between ACE mentors and a pupil's family has proved to be a lever for success with TKAT schools. This involves mentors regularly engaging with home to share the goals that have been agreed and how the pupil is making progress towards these. This approach is based on research by Sime and Sheridan (2014) that examines the value of parental engagement as a means of supporting children to overcome poverty-related barriers to learning.

Mentors should work closely with parents and carers to help families understand the goals pupils have and the ways in which school and home can overcome some of the challenges that might exist to these goals. This has proved useful in helping to support parents in understanding what their child has achieved and what they are capable of further achieving in relation to their academic studies. Sime and Sheridan (2014) suggest that this shared partnership dynamic between home and school can support parents to become more confident in their parenting abilities and involved in their child's education.

Enrichment opportunities

Enabling pupils to take part in more enrichment activities has proved a useful way of supporting pupils to grow in confidence and overcome some of the obstacles that poverty or social exclusion can create to participation.

Example: A pupil wanted to take part in a school trip but was anxious about asking family because of the financial burden it might create. The ACE mentor was able to work with colleagues in the school to secure the pupil a place on the trip and to help ensure it was affordable for the family. Parents were anxious about their child attending the trip until they discovered that the ACE mentor would also be present.

Share practice and success

Ongoing CPD has proved vital to ensuring that adults in schools have the expertise needed to both understand barriers to learning and facilitate a pupil's chances of overcoming them.

TKAT introduced an in-house accredited status for ACE mentors who had completed the core training. This has allowed for greater consistency but has also proved helpful in developing the school workforce. Schools make use of supervision sessions in which ACE mentors meet with a facilitator to discuss their successes and challenges from ACE mentoring in practice. This provides support to tutors and helped develop ACE mentoring across each of the schools.

Many ACE mentors have transitioned from teaching assistant and support staff roles because it has enabled them to work more closely and purposefully with individual pupils facing significant barriers to learning. TKAT has introduced an apprenticeship programme to support adults with limited qualifications to become qualified ACE mentors too. This supports with both the recruitment and the retention of staff across all of the TKAT schools.

Growing ACE in other settings

ACE tutors do not subscribe to the idea that quick fixes or easy solutions exist to many of the challenges that pupils face. However, the principle of championing pupils to understand challenges, identify goals and work together to overcome barriers to learning is one that every school can support. TKAT has been successful in securing funding to further support with the implementation of ACE mentoring in other schools. TKAT is also willing to work alongside any other

Mentoring

schools to understand ACE mentoring and how school leaders can make it a reality for their pupils.

School leaders and teachers may want to make use of the reflection activities provided in this chapter to further consider how the ACE approach can be understood in other settings.

To develop ACE approaches in their own settings, schools can adopt several practical ideas:

1. **Implement regular ACE tutoring:** Ensure every pupil, especially those facing poverty-related barriers to learning, has regular one-to-one sessions with an ACE tutor, tailored to their needs and goals. TKAT works with schools nationally on supporting an understanding of ACE and how to implement this.

2. **Adapt to individual needs:** Use a structured approach like Red, Amber, Green (RAG) ratings to tailor ACE tutoring frequency based on individual pastoral and academic needs. This helps to ensure that staff understand actual barriers to learning that might exist because of poverty and disadvantage, as opposed to assuming these about pupils.

3. **Foster parental engagement:** Encourage active parental involvement through regular updates and face-to-face interactions, creating a supportive home–school partnership. Many schools will already have these processes in place, but it is important to find other ways of doing it that do not rely on these conversations only taking place at parents' evenings – for example, regular phone calls home, weekly check-ins to provide updates of when pupils have achieved something well, timely communication through personal emails and using parental communication systems in school.

4. **Seek funding and collaboration:** Explore avenues for securing funding to support ACE implementation, leveraging success stories and collaboration opportunities with organisations like TKAT for guidance and support.

By championing a holistic approach to student support, schools can nurture an environment where pupils feel empowered to identify and overcome barriers, fostering a positive impact on their learning and wellbeing.

Chapter takeaways

- Develop a comprehensive training programme for mentors to equip them with skills in identifying specific challenges and barriers that might exist because of poverty or disadvantage. Include strategies on how to effectively address these barriers through personalised support plans.
- Facilitate a structured process where mentors and pupils collaboratively set achievable goals. It is important that these are recorded and continuously revisited. It might take time to establish them, but ensure that they are understood by mentor and pupil.
- Parental engagement and partnership is an important part of the relationship. Establish robust communication channels between mentors and parents/carers to foster a supportive partnership.
- Every PP pupil in TKAT has access to an ACE mentor and meets with them regularly. This might not be possible with your school immediately, so prioritise where there are known and acute needs for pupils facing poverty-related barriers.
- Regular support and CPD for ACE mentors has been an important part of ensuring success for the programme. Provide training on strategies for overcoming common challenges, and workshops on topics relevant to student welfare and academic progress.

Recap and Reflective tasks

Recap

Indicate which statements are true or false based on your understanding.	True	False
TKAT ACE is essentially a pastoral mentoring programme.		
ACE mentoring can be readily used in one-to-one and small-group contexts.		
Parental engagement is likely to be a barrier for some disadvantaged pupils and therefore should be considered as an optional component.		
ACE mentoring is built on the belief that most disadvantaged pupils and their families have low aspirations.		
ACE tutors focus on identifying barriers to learning and helping pupils to overcome these. This can take a significant amount of time.		

Reflective tasks

Reflective task for school leaders and teachers
What are the common issues faced by pupils in your school? Which of these are most urgent? Why?
What is the school doing to address these issues currently? How could one-to-one mentoring, using the principles of ACE, further support and develop these approaches?

Tackling Poverty and Disadvantage in Schools

Introducing the principles of ACE
How could you introduce a one-to-one programme of mentoring for pupils facing disadvantage to the school's leadership and staff to ensure there is a clear understanding and support for the programme?

Developing mentors
Consider your reading of the chapter. How could your school develop staff to take on the role of one-to-one mentors and to adopt the approach explored in this chapter?

Next steps
What are the questions and ideas you have about one-to-one mentoring in your setting, based on your reading of this chapter? Please do consider reaching out to colleagues at TKAT to share your ideas and to explore how the schools might be able to support your design of ACE.

 Further reading

Cavell et al. (2021) – 'Back to the future: Mentoring as means and end in promoting child mental health'
Luo and Stoeger (2023) – 'Unlocking the transformative power of mentoring for youth development in communities, schools, and talent domains'

Links

ImpactEd: www.evaluation.impactedgroup.uk
TKAT ACE Mentoring – our dedicated website also features further case studies and a video that illustrates the impact that ACE mentoring has had on one pupil and his family: https://sites.google.com/chs-tkat.org/tkat-ace/home
Mental Health in Schools Insights (Leeds Beckett University's Carnegie School of Education): www.leedsbeckett.ac.uk/research/carnegie-centre-of-excellence-for-mental-health-in-schools/working-paper-series

13 Engagement with business and industry

Katrina Morley

Chapter summary

For children facing poverty-related barriers to learning, there is a heightened risk of being NEET (not in education, employment or training) or being unemployed throughout their life. Additionally, they have a higher probability of accessing lower-skilled roles, which are less well-paid and often perpetuate a poverty cycle. Therefore, this chapter explores the need for careers-related learning (CRL) which is delivered through a planned curriculum, and – crucially – starts in the primary phase.

Fundamentally, children and young people cannot recognise, relate to or become something if they don't know that it exists or have the skills to access it.

What does the research suggest?

In this section, we have provided a brief summary of the research that has helped us in developing a 'classroom to careers' curriculum provision offer for pupils in the Tees Valley. The studies highlight how barriers like limited learning environments, career-related learning, and stark disparities in post-education outcomes compound over time, perpetuating cycles of inequality. The research helps to outline the critical role of schools in breaking down barriers and fostering long-term success. It is not simply a case of raising aspirations. So many of these young people do have aspirations, but structural and persistent inequalities mean that access to opportunities can be limited. It is this that schools, in partnership with other sectors, must understand, navigate and address.

Research 1

Clarke and Thévenon (2022), OECD papers on Wellbeing and Inequalities, No. 04

'Starting unequal: How's life for disadvantaged children?'

This research looks at how living in poverty means being exposed to a range of individual but related barriers, building upon earlier chapters. It then notes that over a lifetime, these barriers compound and often limit employment opportunities. Being unemployed or in low-skilled roles over your life perpetuates the poverty cycle, so it is important for schools to ask which learning and habits could help in breaking down some of the barriers and provide greater opportunity for all.

Key points

- Children from disadvantaged backgrounds frequently experience poorer-quality learning environments, are more likely to experience bullying and more often report a lack of connectedness to their school and others.

- This affects attendance in school and creates gaps in knowledge, leading to slower progress and lower attainment, which ultimately affects their qualifications, skill levels and confidence. In turn this limits their employability and capacity to earn.

- Children from disadvantaged backgrounds more often grow up in poorer-quality local areas, increasing their exposure to crime and placing limits on their opportunities to socialise and participate in community life.

- They are therefore less likely to see and experience a range of life opportunities, negatively impacting upon their development of a range of soft skills, as well as limiting their range of social and cultural capital. Once again, this can potentially have an impact on their employability.

Research 2

Kashefpakdel et al. (2018)

'What works? Career-related learning in primary schools'

Commissioned by the Careers Enterprise Company (CEC), this national study provides evidence of the benefits of career-related learning (CRL) for all children in primary school, but especially those from disadvantaged areas. It recognises that it is too late to expect either all or the bulk of CRL to take place over a child's secondary and further education phases.

The term CRL includes a variety of opportunities to find out about, experience, work with and apply aspects of the world of work as part of the existing curriculum, including subject learning. This research helped to support the government to launch primary careers education at the beginning of 2023 and also underpinned the careers-related curriculum that is currently offered by Tees Valley Education (TVEd).

Key points

The positive outcomes of a good CRL offer can manifest in various ways. Examples include:

- enhanced confidence and self-awareness amongst children, their families and teaching staff

- better understanding of the connections between education, qualifications, skills and future work prospects, which helps early preparation for adulthood

- opportunities to identify and address stereotypes and barriers

- development of a realistic understanding of different occupations available and the associated local, regional or national skills needed to access them

- better support and development of families' attitudes to, perceptions of and knowledge regarding their children's educational and career choices.

Research 3

Teach First (2022)

'Stark destination gap: Disadvantaged pupils twice as likely to be out of work or education as their wealthier peers'

The research contributing to this article looks at the longitudinal risks to disadvantaged children's employability and subsequent life pathways, in comparison to their non-disadvantaged peers. The national comparison of the lived reality of the young people shows how the consequences of poverty can, and often do, last a lifetime.

Key points

Headlines from the research include:

- One in three (33 per cent) young people from disadvantaged backgrounds are not engaged in sustained education, apprenticeships or employment five years after completing their GCSEs, compared to only one in seven (14 per cent) of their non-disadvantaged peers.

- Pupils identified as disadvantaged (33 per cent) are more likely to be out of sustained education or employment than they are to attend university (27 per cent), showcasing a significant disparity in post-GCSE outcomes based on socioeconomic background.

- Over time, the gap in sustained destinations between pupils facing disadvantage and other pupils widens: one year after GCSEs, the gap is eight per cent; three years after, it grows to 14 per cent; and by five years, the gap reaches 19 per cent.

- There are clear disparities and challenges faced by pupils experiencing disadvantage and poverty-related barriers to learning in achieving sustained educational and employment outcomes compared to their more affluent peers.

Other useful research

There are limited studies around CRL and most link back to the Careers and Enterprise Company; however, broader reading around social mobility, access to ambition and how to build up skilled workforces is covered below.

- **Kashefpakdel et al. (2019)** Career-related learning in primary: This research recommends that primary schools should adopt an approach to career-related learning that allows pupils to progressively engage with a variety of experiences related to education, transitions and the world of work, starting from as early as the age of five.

- **McMahon and Watson (2022)** 'Career development learning in childhood: This research is helpful for outlining why career-related knowledge and skills in childhood are foundational for lifelong career development and promoting academic success. The research advocates for greater collaboration between theory, research and practice in developing effective career development programmes for children, aiming to enhance educational outcomes and societal equity.

Case Study

Tees Valley Education – Year 6 sustainability project

As part of the existing CRL curriculum at TVEd, Year 6 pupils collaborate with Teesside University leaders to design a futuristic and sustainable version of their local town that links to the UNESCO sustainability goals. Introduced through a video briefing, and resembling challenges from *The Apprentice*, pupils present their final ideas to a panel of judges.

The project brief was designed between teachers at Tees Valley Education with academics at the International Business School (Teesside University). It also had industry sector partners contributing to the brief, as well as actually working with the pupils in the delivery of the presentation. The project focuses on the concepts of sustainability and innovation, with pupils also having to consider the unique selling points (USPs) of their project design.

Teachers and leaders initially believed that pupils would focus on creating a paper-based project design. However, pupils interpreted and implemented the project using a range of technology and creative media design ideas.

Their concepts included street-cleaning robots, vegan-friendly outlets and ideas for creating sustainable energy options locally. Some of the pupils presented their project designs using Minecraft, showcasing virtual versions of their local town. The project's success earned it recognition as a UNESCO case study.

This project incorporates curriculum links across STEM, geography, computing, coding and mathematics. Reading, writing and oracy skills feature heavily too, because pupils have to work in teams, engage with sector experts and undertake certain roles within the project, as well as prepare and deliver a pitch as part of their project. Visiting a university, being immersed in the International Business School and meeting pupils, academics and entrepreneurs further adds value to the experience. It roots subject learning into the real world on their doorstep. The project ensures that all pupils continue to have meaningful encounters with their local businesses and industry groups, as well as fostering their curiosity, soft skill development, creative application and problem-solving skills. It increases the children's confidence, engages the parents and broadens the awareness of local opportunities to learn and earn.

This particular project builds upon learning mapped as a part of the TVEd Key Stage 2 careers-related learning curriculum offer. Other projects within this have included a river and global shipping focus, as well as entrepreneurial business start-ups.

Maritime Futures

Maritime Futures is an integrated curriculum approach at Key Stage 3, pioneered by Cowes Enterprise College on the Isle of Wight. In discrete curriculum subjects such as maths, science, geography, history and art, National Curriculum content is taught through a maritime lens, using the wealth of applied learning opportunities across the local maritime sector. The curriculum is therefore firmly rooted in the hyperlocal context of the Isle of Wight.

Curriculum leaders work together so that learning in each discipline reinforces and enhances the learning in and across other subjects, in order for pupils to apply their knowledge to practical projects. For example, pupils build boats in design and technology and apply what they have learned on the physics of buoyancy, drag and variables. Local maritime employers advise on curriculum content and help deliver some lessons.

The best way to understand Maritime Futures is to look at the high-level curriculum journey provided for free on the Maritime Futures website (link provided at the end of the chapter).

The success that Cowes Enterprise College has had with their CRL curriculum is currently being used to support Tees Valley Education Trust and the associated local maritime businesses in co-designing a bespoke maritime curriculum for primary-aged pupils. The college has been successful in accessing additional funding to support other schools and organisations in developing CRL curriculum opportunities for pupils.

School leaders and teachers wanting to find out more about this support can contact the college through the further links provided at the end of the chapter.

 Ideas to try

At Tees Valley Education, we have also sought to ensure that CRL sits within our social justice charter (explored in Chapter 1) and our commitment to tackling poverty-related barriers to learning. Our academies serve communities in the North of England who face significant socioeconomic disadvantage. However, the regions we serve are also witnessing some changes to both the scope and volume of employment opportunities. The growth of a range of industries around the port, including logistics, fabrication and renewable energy as well as the digital and creative sectors, is significant.

This means that our pupils have potentially exciting opportunities ahead of them in careers and industry. However, as school leaders and teachers we recognise that this comes with a further challenge. Some of the aforementioned research indicates that there are often many poverty-related barriers to understanding and accessing this industry for both pupils and families.

Whilst some of the opportunities and challenges in your particular locality will look different, take the time to get to know exactly what they are. Along with the research around the need for a CRL offer, the gathering of localised intelligence was a starting point for both of the case studies here. We hope, therefore, that the material below will help equip you with a route map to creating an intentional and locally effective CRL curricula.

Understanding local industry and business

A sound knowledge of local industry and infrastructure is important for the effective delivery of a CRL curriculum if teachers are expected to help pupils understand it. Leaders and teachers may have limited prior industry experience or be unfamiliar with local industries beyond the education sector.

Some of the ways in which we have helped to address this as a MAT include:

- We deliberately join business forums and form partnerships with local industries and businesses. Learning about their specific needs as well as understanding the investments in the area means a good local intelligence.
- We facilitate focus group discussions with families and residents who have lived and worked in the local community for significant amounts of time. This can be useful for understanding more about how industry has changed and what local people deem to be their main options for employment in the area.
- We regularly feature a spotlight on specific industries, businesses and careers in our academy newsletters. We interview colleagues working in other industries and then summarise their roles and reflections as part of a trust-wide magazine to families, staff and our communities.
- On the Trust governance board, we are deliberate about ensuring a range of business sectors and industries are represented. This means that our leaders are regularly encouraged to think beyond the education sector and access learning available from other industries.

Collaboration with hyperlocal business and industry

Local business and industry engagement is important to us as a MAT because we have identified that poverty-related barriers exist in a number of areas, such as with transport and accessing industries further afield for families. By understanding those industries and career opportunities that exist within the immediate vicinity of the communities that we serve, we are demonstrating that you can stay local but still access global opportunity, all whilst earning and learning. This concept delivers far-reaching opportunities, as it engenders confidence and belief in the pupils and the families of genuinely being able to access them. Earning whilst learning and investing in skill growth over a lifetime is a pathway for all.

Therefore, begin by carefully mapping what local industry exists and which industries or businesses could be potential partners for your academies to work with.

Consider the following steps to develop these partnerships:

- Signpost local industry and business to what you are doing – routinely use social media (e.g. LinkedIn) to promote and celebrate stories of interest with local industry, including careers in your communities. This could be publications you are involved in, CRL days in the school, visits to the children from different industries or employment pathways, trips out to local businesses, sponsorship opportunities or interactions where businesses use their corporate social responsibility strategy to help your school.

- Invite local industry and business leaders to present awards to pupils and staff as part of academy/school celebration events.

- Consider becoming a member of local business and enterprise forums. MAT leaders both attend the two main forums in the locality and it helps them to be informed about local business endeavours, partnerships and funding opportunities, which then help to shape our CRL in academies. This is particularly important in primary, as more typically it has been colleges and HE leaders attending.

Collaboration on curriculum

Many of the industries and businesses that we have worked with are generous with their expertise, resources and time. As school leaders and teachers, we have a responsibility to work in collaboration with these colleagues to identify and map the CRL curriculum.

At TVEd, we worked with a group of maritime industry leaders to learn what they needed to see in their workforce, what they wanted parents and the community to know about them and therefore what was special about their business. The Trust then went away to plan the maritime CRL subject curriculum, but also included this specific learning within the offer. An interactive process of then sharing and editing the draft curriculum, with constant feedback and challenge from industrial partners, happened over the course of two terms. This co-creation meant that local identity, domain-specific knowledge and industrial links for the present day and the future offered a far richer curriculum for the pupils.

The following have been levers for successful co-design of the CRL curriculum:

- Ensure that senior leaders within the school who have a responsibility for CRL (typically deputy head level upwards) have regular exposure to business, industry and enterprise opportunities locally. Details of these groups can be found from regional chambers of commerce, regional combined authorities, local business forums (often on social media), local universities and your own local knowledge of the area.

- Work with pupils and teachers at an individual school level to find out what is already known about local industry and the career ambitions pupils have. We use a blend of pupil voice, research surveys and teacher feedback to routinely reflect on these topics. It helps our teachers to understand what pupils do and do not know, instead of making assumptions.

- Once you've identified a specific local focus and growth industry, share your CRL curriculum planning with industry and business leaders. This will help you to sharpen your curriculum content and revise ideas based on feedback, as well as support CSR involvement as a community.

Concept mapping

The idea of conceptual development in curriculum design is explored more fully in Chapter 7. To help design and develop our CRL offer to pupils, our school leaders and teachers began by mapping the core concepts we wanted our children to learn. These are likely to change and need revision over time based on industry trends and feedback. You can read more about these by exploring our CRL curriculum overview (see the link section).

1. Map what you want pupils to learn

Teachers, working in collaboration with their leaders who have gathered local industry knowledge, map the concepts we want pupils to learn. This helps our pupils to learn knowledge about local industries but it also supports personal development pathways for pupils, because it inevitably helps them begin to form a language about employability.

2. Map the skills you want pupils to learn

Following this, leaders and teachers map subject content knowledge alongside the skills we want pupils to learn. Each concept is supported by a specific project-based applied learning opportunity, which involves pupils having a meaningful encounter with industry and business in the community. We believe that this supports the confidence and long-term memory of our pupils. Furthermore, it means that pupils facing poverty-related barriers have multiple planned opportunities to understand and access industry in their local community.

Chapter takeaways

- School leaders and teachers can collaborate with local industry and businesses to create CLR curriculum opportunities, aiming to tackle poverty-related barriers and facilitate awareness of and access to industries for *all* pupils and families.

- Consider the local businesses and industries which will be meaningful for pupils and families in the context of your school community. This helps pupils to understand what exists locally and accessible routes into these sectors and industries.

- Collaboration with local industry and business is important for supporting the growth of teacher expertise in CRL and providing robust curriculum opportunities for pupils, especially those with limited experiences due to poverty and disadvantage.

- Be clear on the concepts and encounters that CRL curriculum opportunities will offer pupils. Meaningful encounters and project-based approaches to learning will have a greater impact that a standalone event.

⊞ Recap and Reflective tasks

Recap

Indicate which statements are true or false based on your understanding.	True	False
Pupils facing poverty-related barriers to learning should have the opportunity to engage with and understand a diverse range of local roles from business and industry.		
Recent research emphasises the need for collaborative efforts amongst educators, policymakers and businesses to address skills gaps and ensure that disadvantaged pupils receive preparation for future employment opportunities.		
Research reveals that establishing a careers-related learning programme for primary school children does not have a significant impact, particularly for the most disadvantaged individuals.		

Reflective tasks

Reflective task for leaders and teacher educators
Consider your reading of this chapter and the CRL opportunities that pupils currently have in your school. • Summarise why CRL in your curriculum is important for your pupils. *Try to make the relationship between CRL and the values/ethos of the school explicit. Further information about linking curriculum to school culture can be explored in Chapters 7 and 8.*

Consider your reading of this chapter and the CRL opportunities that pupils currently have in your school.

- Summarise why CRL in your curriculum is important for your pupils.
  Try to make the relationship between CRL and the values/ethos of the school explicit. Further information about linking curriculum to school culture can be explored in Chapters 7 and 8.

- Consider your local context. Who are the main business and industry partners who could support the development of CRL opportunities for pupils in your school(s)?

- Consider how you will approach these partners. You might find it helpful to refer to Chapter 11 on forming partnerships with other organisations and make use of the Theory of Change reflective task.

Reflective task for teachers/curriculum leaders	
Concepts Consider the key concepts and skills that you want pupils to understand in relation to local business, industry and enterprise in your school(s).	
Concept	
Skills	

Next, consider the ways in which links could be made with existing curriculum content in subject areas. An example is provided for you.

Concept	Innovation
Skills	• Product design • Forming an argument • Producing a storyboard • Producing a project workplan
Curriculum links	Design and technology: Pupils currently design their own ideas for a school bag. They have to consider the unique selling points (USPs) of this. English: Pupils use persuasive writing to write a newspaper article advertising a new product or idea.

Next, consider a project that pupils could engage with alongside a local business/industry partner to help make this learning a meaningful encounter in CRL. You may find it helpful to explore some of the resources provided by Maritime Futures on their website and in the digital resource area via the link provided at the end of the chapter.

Project idea outline:	Potential business/industry partners who might help to support this:

Finally, consider pitching this idea to the following to invite further scrutiny of the idea and refine your idea(s) accordingly.

- Senior leadership team and/or leader responsible for CRL in school
- A small group of curriculum leaders and/or teachers
- One or more local business and industry representatives
- Pupils and parents: Consider the extent to which there is an interest in the project and what they may like to gain from the project(s).

📖 Further reading

Croll (2008) – 'Occupational choice, socioeconomic status and educational attainment: A study of the occupational choices and destinations of young people in British Household Panel Survey'

Department for Education (2023) – 'How we are helping to inspire primary school children about their future careers'

Education and Employers (2010) – 'The point of partnership: The case for employer engagement in education'

Flouri and Panourgia (2012) – 'Do primary school children's career aspirations matter? The relationship between family, poverty, career aspirations, and emotional and behavioural problems'

Kashefpakdel and Percy (2016) – 'Career education that works: An economic analysis using the British Cohort Study'

OECD (2021b) – 'The future at five: Gendered aspirations of five-year-olds'

Teach First (2024) – 'UK STEM skills shortage "at risk of growing" as low-income parents fear for children's prospects'

Links

Maritime Futures: https://maritimefutures.co.uk

Tees Valley Education – classroom to careers curriculum: www.teesvalleyeducation.co.uk/trust-specialisms/business-enterprise

14 Research collaboration
Professor Dorothy Newbury-Birch, Sean Harris

Chapter summary

The complexity of poverty and disadvantage in communities is too significant for schools to respond in silos. In this chapter, we explore the ways in which schools can forge partnerships with universities and other research organisations to both understand and tackle poverty.

 What does the research suggest?

We have highlighted examples of research that frames some of the reasons why strategic partnerships with universities are important for schools in tackling poverty.

Research 1

Newbury-Birch and Allan (2020)

Co-Creating and Co-Producing Research Evidence: A Guide for Practitioners and Academics in Health, Social Care and Education Settings
Research co-produced by academics and practitioners from early stages to end results can have important benefits. Newbury-Birch and Allan produced this guide for researchers to understand more about the principles of co-production research and the ways in which this can be implemented in settings.

Pupils in a secondary school wanted to work alongside academics at Teesside University and alongside teachers in their school. The school was situated in an area of significant socioeconomic disadvantage. Pupils chose to focus on the topic of recent GCSE reforms and the impact that changes to GCSE outcome measures was having on the school. The case study provided researchers, teachers and pupils with an experience of how co-production can benefit multiple stakeholders in schools. Many of the pupils described how engaging in the research helped them to understand opportunities that could be accessed in HE.

Key points

Some of the recommendations that emerged from this study include:

- Ensure that research staff have the correct checks in place to be allowed to work in the school.
- Pupils should be involved from the inception to the dissemination of the research project.
- Allocate research tasks appropriately by considering individual strengths, so that all members of the research team feel valued.
- Good communication is imperative. Being clear from the outset of the expectations and requirements of pupils and staff makes a research project run more smoothly.
- Training and support are important to build both research skills and confidence; it is important that this is pitched at an appropriate level for children and young people in schools.
- Ensure that everybody is treated equally and able to get their opinions across – reinforce that no question is a stupid question in schools or research!

Research 2

Montacute and Cullinane (2023)

'25 years of university access: How access to higher education has changed over time'

Montacute and Cullinane produced this report through The Sutton Trust, highlighting higher education trends over the past two decades. According to the research, the progress that has been made in closing access gaps between state and independent school pupils has not translated into significantly more equal representation of young people from less advantaged homes.

Key points

- The report shows that whilst we have more pupils accessing HE than ever, an escalating education 'arms race' has meant that narrowing the gaps in access to the most selective universities has been stubbornly slow.

- According to the research, 4,700 state school pupils and 1,000 pupils from areas of the country with low historic participation are 'missing' from the 30 most selective universities each year – these young people have the required grades but don't get places.

- The report adds further weight to research indicating the value of schools and universities working together to understand context and the barriers that exist for both pupils and families in accessing HE.

Research 3

Leat et al. (2015)

'Teachers' experiences of engagement with and in educational research: What can be learned from teachers' views?'

This research paper is useful for leaders and teachers wanting to understand what is known about teachers' engagement in and with educational research. The paper draws on international contexts and a range of insights from teachers on the benefits of engaging with research.

Although the paper does not specifically study educational disadvantage or inequality, it emphasises how important it is for teachers to engage in dialogues and take proactive roles in their schools. The researchers suggest that when teachers have access to research support, they can hear from university experts and read articles and books that offer different perspectives. This exposure helps teachers develop a more nuanced understanding of their classrooms and schools.

Key points

The research cites a range of benefits for school-based practitioners working alongside academic researchers in the research process.

- They argue that teachers learn well about research through engaging in the research process.

- This is particularly the case where projects are sustained and there is an iterative dimension to learning.

Other useful research

- **Bakhtiar et al. (2023):** A systematic review of peer-reviewed research relating to children aged 15 and under as researchers. The review may inform children's participation in broader areas such as service, environmental or curriculum design and policy reviews.

- **Wang and Zhang (2014):** According to this research, in effective university–school partnerships, teachers can receive constructive guidance and scaffolding from university researchers and teacher educators, which can help enhance their research knowledge and skills and enable them to absorb new ideas about language teaching and learning.

- **Burn et al. (2016):** This research reaffirms the value of school and university partnerships, particularly in relation to supporting novice or early career teachers in understanding issues linked to social justice.

Research takeaways

- Poverty and disadvantage are too complex for schools to attempt to understand or tackle in isolation. This can be supported by research expertise and resources.

- Partnerships with universities and other research organisations can help to provide a strategic response to understanding community need and how to tackle it.

- Research indicates that persistent gaps exist for pupils facing disadvantage or poverty-related barriers to learning in terms of access to university/higher education.

Case Study

The following case study outlines an example of a research project designed in collaboration with schools and other organisations.

Tackling Poverty and Disadvantage in Schools

SHINE: Crafting curriculum with poverty in mind

Two academies in Tees Valley Education (TVEd) applied for the Let Teachers SHINE grant with the charity SHINE. The Let Teachers SHINE fund offers grants of up to £25,000 over two years, plus dedicated support from a hands-on funder. SHINE seeks to support teachers with innovative ideas for projects that can be trialled and developed with the potential to improve outcomes for socioeconomically disadvantaged pupils.

A grant of £18,000 from SHINE has supported teachers at TVEd with researching the common misconceptions that exist in a range of curriculum subjects for pupils facing poverty-related barriers to learning. Teachers have used the funding to access teacher education and CPD provided by Evidence Based Education (EBE) and the Chartered College of Teaching (CCoT). This has supported teachers to understand more about the principles of effective planning and diagnosing pupil misconceptions as part of teacher planning.

The action-research project and strategy involves anticipating potential difficulties that pupils, especially those from low-income backgrounds, may encounter and incorporating the pupils' perspectives to inform the design and implementation of the curriculum. The aim of this approach is to create a more meaningful and engaging learning experience for all pupils in the academies.

The research collaborative with SHINE, EBE and the CCoT has helped project leaders and teachers understand research principles and better approaches to project implementation. It is also supporting teachers in accessing a range of journals, research papers and virtual learning, which supports with curriculum implementation in classrooms. The project has been highlighted in national case studies and has prompted teachers to share their project insights at conferences held both regionally and nationally.

 Ideas to try

In this section we briefly outline some of the practical considerations that you as school leaders and teachers may wish to consider before setting out to collaborate on research project design and implementation.

Research design and implementation

We have been involved with research projects that have sought to support schools by involving pupils and teachers actively in research. These are some principles to consider as part of designing a small-scale research project alongside pupils and researchers.

- **Find a focus:** Work with pupils to identify a topic that is going to be of interest in specific school contexts. Then consider the research question(s) that will underpin this.

- **Find a volunteer army:** Identify adults and pupils that can implement the project at scale.

- **Find your research partnership:** Reflection activities have been provided at the end of this chapter to support you with the process of research design. Once you have started to use these tools, consider which HE partnerships will add value to the research project.

Working with pupils as researchers

Working with pupils in research contexts can be immensely rewarding, but it can present challenges. They need to be at the heart of all decisions. Projects that we have facilitated with pupils as researchers have benefited from the following:

- **Co-production:** Find out what pupils want to know more about. Involve pupils in the design. This might include working with pupils in the initial design phase of the research and asking them to indicate what type of problems or issues they would like to investigate. Invite pupils to suggests ways that they might want to investigate or find out more about these topics. This might lead to pupils sharing or identifying approaches that have not previously been considered by research teams or the school.

- **Contracting:** Introduce pupils and staff to research ethics and the need for contracting confidentiality. Safeguarding and child protection policies must be followed.

- **Conduct:** It is important for children and young people to understand that research does not necessarily follow the same protocol as classroom learning. Identify the behaviours and group expectations needed. We encourage pupils working with research academics on a first name basis to help create a culture of adults and pupils working as colleagues.

- **Logistics:** Make sure that any research is done in the context of timings and logistical arrangements that will support pupils and teachers. Meeting outside of regular school hours can be helpful for ensuring that meetings are not compromised or members distracted.

- **Main contact:** Ensure that there is a single point of contact in the school who can hold the thread between external research partnerships and stakeholders internally.

Funding research

For teachers or school leaders with limited experience of applying for funding, the task of identifying and writing bids can be challenging. Some of the dos and don'ts of bid-writing to consider include:

Do	Do not
• **Clarity:** Avoid too much jargon and don't assume that the grant providers will understand the complexity of the problem that you seek to address. Be clear on what your focus is and why. • **Partnership:** Place emphasis on the other partnerships that you are working with. This shows a commitment to scalability of the project(s) and an ability to deliver on the implementation plan. • **Potential impact:** State expected outcomes and impact, and disseminate plans within and beyond the immediate school community. • **Add value:** Be specific on the ways in which the funding and research will not only add value to the school but to the lives of pupils and families too. Make this clear in your application.	• **Copy and paste:** Each funding stream will have a distinct purpose and criteria. You will repeat content for multiple applications, but ensure that the bid is specific to what you are applying for and the grant giver you are approaching. • **Work in isolation:** Make sure that you are considering the volunteer army internally that will help you deliver on the project. State who this is as part of the bid and as part of your implementation planning. • **Over-promise:** Be mindful that schools are complex and demanding organisations. Aim high, but think carefully about the ability of the team(s) to deliver on what is being proposed. • **Just send it:** Always invite a colleague to proofread and sense-check the application prior to sending it.

Facilitate 'fireside' conversations

In our teams, we create opportunities to not only engage with others' research but also to consider what the research means in our contexts. Creating 'fireside' conversations for colleagues to come together as a collective is an important part of sense-checking and applying research. Reflection activities are provided at the end of this chapter to support school leaders and teacher-educators in facilitating these in their own school(s). Two examples are provided below of how school leaders can further develop this principle.

Team Alpha

Team Alpha is a research team based at Teesside University. Dorothy leads this team, which consists of a range of academic research practitioners from multiple sectors.

- The team engages in a weekly review meeting, whereby pupils and research academics are able to bring aspects of research thinking or projects that they are working on.
- Colleagues are invited to be critical friends and to ask questions about the research.
- The team also facilitates regular webinars and invites thinkers from other sectors to present on topics that encourage further research reflection and skills development in the team (e.g. developing networking, managing work-related stress and demands).

Virtual Learning Community

At TVEd, all staff have access to a Virtual Learning Community (VLC).

- The VLC is an online collaborative space in which weekly research updates are circulated related to pedagogy or aspects of educational disadvantage.
- Following this, research and development clusters are used to further facilitate discussions about reading that has been circulated.
- Using a 3-2-1 approach to these conversations can provide a helpful prompt:

  - **Three** insights or headlines from the research paper or book that have stood out to colleagues and reasons for this
  - **Two** possible actions or ideas that colleagues have about their areas of practice in school as a result of this reading

- **One** specific question or query that colleagues have about the research and which would be useful to discuss with other colleagues.

Coping with the challenges of research collaboration

There are challenges with collaborative working and research partnerships between schools, universities and other research settings. Academics and school leaders serve in demanding sectors and, at times, will be working in different cultures and with competing priorities.

- It is important for researchers, academics and those working in schools to recognise the nuances and caveats that surface from working in these different spheres of influence.
- Be realistic about what can be achieved and ensure that all stakeholders are aware of the ebbs and flows of different project timescales within the context of the different organisations.
- Greany and Brown (2015) highlight the importance of universities and schools being transparent about project expectations and what both parties can realistically offer. This has to be at the forefront of any contracting or scoping of partnerships.

Chapter takeaways

- Collaboration with teachers and pupils in co-productive research yields benefits. It is useful to deliberate on research topics and ensure pupils have a voice in the process.
- Numerous charities and organisations support research projects in schools aimed at tackling poverty-related barriers to learning. However, schools need to allocate sufficient time and resources to identify and pursue these funding opportunities.
- School leaders should facilitate opportunities to validate the relevance of research within specific school contexts.
- Collaboration between research academics and school teachers poses challenges, so it is vital to establish clear expectations and carefully plan project implementations.

Recap

Indicate which statements are true or false based on your understanding.	True	False
Research highlights that in areas of educational complexity, such as working with children and families in poverty, contextualised intervention may be needed to disrupt previously held professional assumptions in schools.		
Research indicates that persistent access gaps for disadvantaged pupils are beginning to reduce since 2010, particularly at the most selective universities.		
Evidence suggests that through university–school partnerships, teachers might enhance their research knowledge and skills in such a way that it can contribute to teacher effectiveness.		
Universities and schools are similar sectors with consistent competing demands; therefore, working together in collaboration is likely to be effortless.		

Reflective tasks

Reflective task for school leaders
Preparing a research project in school List some of the common problems that you face in your school(s) that might be connected to poverty-related barriers to learning or disadvantage.
Leadership reflection Choosing just one of these problems, make a note of some of the questions that might be asked by different stakeholders in your school(s) in response to this problem.

School leaders	Teachers and support staff in classrooms
• What questions would they ask in relation to this problem and its different components?	• What questions would they ask in relation to this problem and its different components?

Identify one or two of the questions that you and colleagues would want to further investigate. Next, invite a colleague or small number of colleagues to consider the implications of these questions.

Why is this a question that we want to answer as teachers and teacher educators?

What might be the benefits to finding out more about this question for our school(s)?

Which organisations or universities locally might be interested in supporting us in co-constructing a way to find out an answer to this question?

Research primer
Use this to blueprint initial ideas you and colleagues have. Then, use this as the basis of a discussion with an academic researcher and/or team in HE to support collaboration and further development of your ideas.

State the problem that you want to investigate as a single research question:

Aims and intent
Identify three to five aims and objectives you would want to fulfil through this project.

Suggestions for design
Prior to pitching this project to other researchers externally or internally, consider any initial ideas you have about the design of your project.

As part of your research design process, consider and note the following:

Who would we need to talk to and investigate as part of this process?

What methods of research are likely to help with this? Why?

What are the timescales of this research? When do we want to have completed it?
What ethical considerations do we need to make regarding the research and process?
What will we do with the findings? How will these be shared and why?

Reflective task for teacher educators

Facilitating a fireside conversation

Use the activities below to prepare for and facilitate a fireside conversation in your own setting around one piece of research or reading.

Summary of key points What are the *main* threads or aspects of the research/reading that I want to explore further?	Questions emerging What are the *main* questions that I have and would want to discuss further in school(s)?

Fireside participants
Considering the above, who would I want to involve in a virtual or physical fireside conversation about these questions?

Preparing the fireside conversation
Use this section to prepare your fireside discussion about the research/reading. Remember to also share a copy of the research/reading with your fireside participants prior to the conversation.

Aims and intent	Logistics
In a sentence, what is the fireside discussion about and why is this useful for colleagues?	Consider the following to help with facilitation: Format (virtual, physical…): What would work best this time?
	Length of fireside discussion: How do you keep it manageable for teachers/leaders with a busy workload?
Identify aims or intentions of the fireside discussion. What do you want to achieve?	
	Outputs: Who will capture outputs and discussion points?
	Facilitating the conversation: Who will facilitate the conversation this time?

Facilitating the fireside discussion
What were the main themes or threads that colleagues unpicked from the reading/research?
What challenges or issues did colleagues have with the reading/research? Why?
What were the benefits of colleagues engaging with this research/reading? Why?
What reflections or points did colleagues have regarding next steps?

What reading/research would further stoke future fireside conversations with this group?

Reflective task for teachers/curriculum leaders

- Consider your reading of the chapter.
- Consider the different aspects of poverty and disadvantage that you want to know more about in the context of your classroom or curriculum area(s).

Next, choose just *one* of these problems or issues that you want to find out more about as a classroom teacher or curriculum leader. It is important to consider the extent to which you can find out about this and what might be workable in your particular school too.

Next, frame this as a specific research question that you would want to investigate as part of your work as a classroom teacher or curriculum leader.

Research question:

Advantages to exploring this research as part of an internal action-research project in my school:	Barriers to exploring this research as part of an internal action-research project in my school:

Who are the other stakeholders that might be interested in supporting you in finding out more about this problem and ways to address it? Be specific where possible.

Internal stakeholders (e.g. pupils, SLT, colleagues, governors):	External stakeholders (e.g. families, charities, universities, other education networks):

Finally, consider your pitch for this project and how it could be designed and implemented through your current role as a classroom teacher and/or curriculum leader.

Pitch to senior leaders and/or headteacher for implementing this project in my school
Project title:

Why I think it matters (in two to three sentences):

Resource I may need to support with implementation:

Benefits to pupils and/or school:

My ask(s):

Pitch to HE/research partnership for collaboration on this project in my school
Project title:

Why I think it matters (in two to three sentences):

Resource I may need to support with implementation:

Benefits to school and partner(s):

My ask(s):

 Further reading

Bolam et al. (2004) – 'Creating and sustaining effective professional learning communities'
Britton et al. (2021) – 'Which university degrees are best for intergenerational mobility?'

Links

Chartered College of Teaching: https://chartered.college
EEF Evidence into Action podcast series: https://educationendowmentfoundation. org.uk/news/new-eef-podcast-using-research-evidence-well-in-education
Evidence Based Education: https://evidencebased.education
SHINE: https://shinetrust.org.uk/what-we-do/let-teachers-shine

The author team

Sean Harris

Social media handles: @SeanHarris_NE / @ThatPovertyGuy

Background: Sean serves as a doctoral researcher affiliated with Teesside University and is Director of PLACE (People, Learning and Community Engagement) at Tees Valley Education, a multi-academy trust in the North of England. As a freelance author and journalist, he frequently explores topics related to educational inequality and strategies for supporting schools in addressing it. With experience in various leadership roles within both education and the charity sectors, Sean's doctoral research focuses on enhancing schools' comprehension of poverty through collaborative efforts with children and young people. He is a Fellow of the Chartered College of Teaching (FCCT).

Chapters: 1, 6, 8, 9, 10, 14

Katrina Morley

Social media handle: @katrina_morley

Background: Katrina began her career in chemical engineering before moving into education. Following a successful career as a teacher, senior leader and headteacher, Katrina became CEO of Tees Valley Education Trust. She holds a variety of regional and national roles with organisations to support leaders and schools to better tackle educational inequality. Katrina is a Fellow of the Chartered College of Teaching (FCCT) and an honorary professor at Teesside University.

Chapters: 1, 9 and 13

Debi Bailey

Social media handles: @BaileyDebi/@NEATschools

Background: Debi has vast experience of working in education in a range of different roles, including headteacher of a large primary school and local authority (LA) literacy consultant, and has inspectorial experience with Ofsted. Alongside her role as Chief Executive Officer (CEO) at NEAT Academy Trust in the North East of England, Debi supports individual school leaders and trusts with school improvement in her role as a national leader of education.

Chapter: 1

Anna Carter

Social media handle: @NPATrust

Background: Anna is Curriculum and Teacher Professional Development Lead at Northampton Primary Academies Trust. She works closely with a wide range of schools and organisations nationally to help school leaders and teachers better understand the complexity of disadvantage and how teacher education can be used to help address it.

Chapter: 2

Julia Kedwards

Social media handle: @NPATrust

Background: Julia is CEO for the Northampton Primary Academies Trust, with a focus on school improvement, learning and teaching, and the development of education. She has held a range of leadership positions in education, including headteacher. Julia is passionate about tackling poverty in communities and believes that education can achieve this.

Chapter: 2

Lorna Nicoll

Social media handle: @povertyproofcne

Background: Lorna is an experienced teacher, senior leader in primary and Early Years settings and school governor. She has worked across the UK and internationally in a wide range of education settings. Lorna has been working with the charity Children North East and their Poverty Proofing© programmes since 2018.

Chapter: 3

Luke Bramhall

Social media handle: @NCLCarers

Background: Luke is an experienced leader and has worked with schools, charities and the third sector in a wide range of roles. He is CEO at Newcastle Carers, a charity that provides a range of practical services and holistic support to those who are caring for someone due to illness, disability, mental ill health or problems linked to addiction. Previously, Luke was instrumental in the inception and development of the Poverty Proofing© the School Day programme.

Chapter: 3

Laura McPhee

Social media handle: @LoughboroughPri

Background: Laura is an experienced education leader. She is a former headteacher of Loughborough Primary School and currently works as Director of Education for University Schools Trust. She is a passionate advocate for social justice and has the privilege of carrying out pro bono consultancy work with charities and other organisations.

Chapter: 4

Shayne Elsworth

Social media handle: @shayneelsworth

Background: Shayne has held several senior leadership positions in a range of school settings across the country and is currently Vice Principal (Curriculum and Outcomes) at Bede Academy in Northumberland, a school in the Emmanuel Schools Foundation. He has written for a number of educational publications and is passionate about place-based change in communities.

Chapter: 5

Sara Davidson

Social media handle: www.linkedin.com/in/sara-davidson-981827300

Background: As Director of Red Kite Education, Sara leads Red Kite Alliance, Teacher Training and the Teaching School Hub, as well as Red Kite Connect. Originally a secondary English teacher, she has a wide range of experience as a middle and senior leader, acting headteacher and as local authority Strategic Lead for Education.

Chapter: 6

Darren Higgins

Background: Darren is a retired headteacher and senior leader. He has also served as an academy improvement leader across Tees Valley Education, supporting academies with the development of curriculum, teaching and learning.

Chapter: 7

Stuart Mayle

Social media handle: @BramblesTVEd

Background: Stuart is the Headteacher of Brambles Primary Academy. He has carried out a range of roles in education, including curriculum leader, senior leader and acting headteacher. Stuart is passionate about research in schools, teacher education and the development of character education for pupils. He works closely with a range of schools nationally and is a Member of the Chartered College of Teaching (MCCT).

Chapter: 7

Louisa Harrop

Social media handle: @LouisaHarrop

Background: Louisa is a Christian distinctiveness advisor with Lichfield Diocese in the Church of England. In this role, she supports school leaders and teachers to develop school values, ethos and a commitment to social justice. Louisa has taught religious education for many years and been a curriculum leader and SEND co-ordinator (SENDCo).

Chapter: 8

Martyn Gordon

Social media handle: @martyngordon

Background: Martyn has worked in education for many years and in both secondary and alternative provision settings. He has held senior leadership and headship positions across the North of England. He is now an executive principal at Northern Leaders Trust, a multi-academy trust serving communities in the North of England.

Chapter: 10

John Smith

Social media handle: @educatinghuman1

Background: John is Director of Partnerships at Royal Grammar School, a large independent school in Newcastle upon Tyne. He designs and delivers educational projects across over 100 schools in the North of England. He has been a maths teacher for 20 years and has previously held leadership roles in teaching and learning.

Chapter: 11

David Linsell

Social media handle: @TKATACE

Background: David is a former headteacher and works as Director of Local Governance, Procedure Support and Communications at The Kemnal Academies Trust (TKAT), a large multi-academy trust of 45 schools in the South and East regions of England. He works closely with schools on the development of the ACE (A Champion for Every Child) mentoring programme.

Chapter: 12

Professor Dorothy Newbury-Birch

Social media handle: @dotbirch

Background: Dorothy is a professor of social justice at Teesside University. She is a well-published academic researcher and works with a range of organisations, schools and professionals internationally to help them use research and co-production to tackle health and social inequality at scale.

Chapter: 14

Acronyms

AP: Alternative Provision

CAF: Common Assessment Framework

CCoT: Chartered College of Teaching

CEC: The Careers and Enterprise Company

CIRCLE: The Centre for Innovation, Research, Creativity and Leadership in Education

CPD: Continuing Professional Development

CRL: Career-Related Learning

EAL: English as an Additional Language

ECF: Early Career Framework

ECT: Early Career Teacher

EEF: Education Endowment Foundation

EOTAS: Education Otherwise Than At School

ESG: Environmental, Social and Governance

FSM: Free School Meals

FTE: Fixed Term Exclusion

HE: Higher Education

IRP: Independent Review Panel

ISLDN: International School Leadership Development Network

ITT: Initial Teacher Training

NPQ: National Professional Qualification

NPQLTD: National Professional Qualification in Leading Teacher Development

OECD: Organisation for Economic Co-operation and Development

PD: Professional Development

PP: Pupil Premium

PRU: Pupil Referral Unit

PSHE: Personal, Social, Health and Economic Education

RSE: Relationships and Sex Education

SEND: Special Educational Needs and Disabilities

SENDCo: SEND Co-ordinator

STEM: Science, Technology, Engineering and Mathematics

UASC: Unaccompanied Asylum-Seeking Child

UNESCO: United Nations Educational, Scientific and Cultural Organization

UNHCR: UN Refugee Agency (formally the United Nations Office of the High Commissioner for Refugees)

UNICEF: United Nations Children's Fund

Bibliography

Action for Children (2022), 'Too little, too late: Early help and early intervention spending in England 2022'. https://media.actionforchildren.org.uk/documents/Too_Little_Too_Late_Report_Final.pdf

Agenda Alliance (2022), 'Pushed out left out: Girls Speak: Final report'. www.agendaalliance.org/documents/128/Girls_Speak_-_Pushed_Out_Left_Out_-_Full_Report.pdf

Ainscow, M., Armstrong, W. A., Hughes, B. C. and Rayner, S. (2023), 'Turning the tide: A study of place-based school partnerships'. Staff College. https://thestaffcollege.uk/publications/turning-the-tide

Ambrose, S., Bridges, M. W., DiPietro, M., Lovett, M. C. and Norman, M. K. (2010), *How Learning Works: Seven Research-Based Principles for Smart Teaching*. Washington: Jossey-Bass.

Andrews, J., Robinson, D. and Hutchinson, J. (2017), 'Closing the gap? Trends in educational attainment and disadvantage'. Education Policy Institute. https://epi.org.uk/wp-content/uploads/2017/08/Closing-the-Gap_EPI-.pdf

Allen, G. (2011), 'Early intervention: The next steps'. Department for Work and Pensions. https://assets.publishing.service.gov.uk/media/5a7b837d40f0b645ba3c4d09/early-intervention-next-steps2.pdf

Arthur, J., Fullard, M. and O'Leary, C. (2022), 'Teaching character education: What works?' Research report. Jubilee Centre for Character and Virtues, University of Birmingham.

Arthur, J., Kristjánsson, K., Harrison, T., Sanderse, W. and Mawson, J. (2017), 'A habit of service: The factors that sustain service'. Jubilee Centre for Character and Virtues, University of Birmingham.

Ashlee, A., Clayton, U., Hmmed, S. and Jose, D. (2022), 'Finding their way: The journey to university for refugee and asylum-seeking young people in Coventry'. University of Warwick and Refugee Education UK. www.reuk.org/_files/ugd/3c7d1c_e528f7be90ef481d8e46ee2aed96f83b.pdf

Baars, S., Shaw, B., Mulcahy, E. and Menzies, L. (2018), 'School cultures and practices: Supporting the attainment of disadvantaged pupils: A qualitative comparison of London and non-London schools'. DfE. https://assets.publishing.service.gov.uk/media/5a7b837d40f0b645ba3c4d09/early-intervention-next-steps2.pdf

Baker, S. and Simpson, M. (2020), *A School Without Sanctions: A New Approach to Behaviour Management*. London: Bloomsbury.

Bakhtiar, A., Lang, M., Shelley, B. and West, M. (2023), 'Research with and by children: A systematic literature review'. *Review of Education*, 11, (1), e3384.

Beeson, M., Wildman, J. M. and Wildman, J. (2024), 'Does tackling poverty related barriers to education improve school outcomes? Evidence from the North East of England'. *Economics Letters*, 236, 111614.

Berkowitz, R., Moore, H., Astor, R. A. and Benbenishty, R. (2016), 'A research synthesis of the associations between socioeconomic background, inequality, school climate, and academic achievement'. *Review of Educational Research*, 87, (2), 425–469.

Blair, C. and Raver, C. C. (2016), 'Poverty, stress, and brain development: New directions for prevention and intervention'. *Academic Pediatrics*, 16, (3), S30–S36.

Bolam, R., McMahon, A., Stoll, L., Thomas, S. and Wallace, M. with Greenwood, A., Hawkey, K., Ingram, M., Atkinson, A. and Smith, M. (2004), 'Creating and sustaining effective professional learning communities'. DfES Publications. https://dera.ioe.ac.uk/id/eprint/5622/1/RR637. pdf

Britton, J., Drayton, E. and van der Erve, L. (2021), 'Which university degrees are best for intergenerational mobility?'. Institute for Fiscal Studies and Sutton Trust. https://assets. publishing.service.gov.uk/media/619bba29e90e0704478a9cbf/Scorecards.pdf

Burn, K., Mutton, T., Thompson, I., Ingram, J., McNicholl, J. and Firth, R. (2016), 'The impact of adopting a research orientation towards use of the Pupil Premium grant in preparing beginning teachers in England to understand and work effectively with young people living in poverty'. *Journal of Education for Teaching*, 42, (4), 434–450.

Buttle UK (2023), 'The state of child poverty 2023: Exploring the changing face of child poverty in a cost-of-living crisis'. https://buttleuk.org/wp-content/uploads/2023/08/State-of-Child-Poverty-2023.pdf

Bywaters, P. and Child Welfare Inequalities Project Team (2020), 'The Child Welfare Inequalities Project: Final report Nuffield Foundation. https://pure.hud.ac.uk/ws/files/21398145/ CWIP_Final_Report.pdf

Cambron-McCabe, N. and McCarthy, M. M. (2005), 'Educating school leaders for social justice'. *Educational Policy*, 19, (1), 201–222.

Cavell, T. A., Spencer, R. and McQuillin, S. D. (2021), 'Back to the future: Mentoring as means and end in promoting child mental health'. *Journal of Clinical Child and Adolescent Psychology*, 50, (2), 281–299.

Centre for Research on Families and Relationships (CRFR) (2017), Can we put the "poverty of aspiration" myth to bed now?' Research briefing 91. www.storre.stir. ac.uk/bitstream/1893/26654/1/Can%20we%20put%20the%20poverty%20of%20 aspirations%20myth%20to%20bed%20now.pdf

Centre for Social Justice (2024a), 'Suspending Reality (Part 1): The crisis of school exclusions and what to do about it'. www.centreforsocialjustice.org.uk/wp-content/uploads/2024/01/ CSJ-Suspending_Reality_Part_1.pdf

Centre for Social Justice (2024b), 'Suspending Reality (Part 2): Exclusion rates and inclusive practice in multi-academy trusts'. www.centreforsocialjustice.org.uk/wp-content/ uploads/2024/01/CSJ-Suspending_Reality_Part_2.pdf

Child of the North (2024a), 'An evidence-based plan for addressing poverty with and through education settings'. Centre for Young Lives. www.n8research.org.uk/media/CoTN_ Poverty_Report_2.pdf

Child of the North (2024b), 'An evidence-based plan for addressing the special educational needs and disabilities (SEND) assessment and support crisis'. Child of the North & Centre for Young Lives. www.n8research.org.uk/download/13900/CotN_SEND-AP_Report_6.pdf

Clarke, C. and Thévenon, O. (2022), 'Starting unequal: How's life for disadvantaged children?'. OECD Papers on Well-being and Inequalities. www.oecd-ilibrary.org/docserver/a0ec330c-en.pdf?expires=1728666834&id=id&accname=guest&checksum=15D53547E906D51F2EACD9A6590E8F77.

Collins, J. (2001), *Good to Great: Why Some Companies Make the Leap... and Others Don't*. London: Random House Business books.

Counsell, C. (2018), 'Taking curriculum seriously'. *Impact*, 4, 6–9.

Cremin, T., Mottram, M., Collins, F., Powell, S. and Safford, K. (2009), 'Teachers as readers: Building communities of readers'. *Literacy*, 43, (1), 11–19.

Croll, P. (2008), 'Occupational choice, socioeconomic status and educational attainment: A study of the occupational choices and destinations of young people in British Household Panel Survey'. *Research Papers in Education*, 23, (3), 243–268.

Cummins, P. and Di Prato, A. (2021), 'The character issue', a School for tomorrow. Research Edition, 1, (3). www.aschoolfortomorrow.com/publications

Darling-Hammond, L., Hyler, M. E. and Garner, M. (2017), *Effective Teacher Professional Development*. Palo Alto, CA: Learning Policy Institute.

Darton, D. and Strelitz, J. (2003), *Tackling UK Poverty and Disadvantage in the Twenty-First Century: An Exploration of the Issues*. London: Joseph Rowntree Foundation.

Davis, J. and Marsh, N. (2020), 'Boys to men: The cost of "adultification" in safeguarding responses to Black boys'. *Critical and Radical Social Work*, 8, (2), 255–259.

Demie, F. (2022), *Understanding the Causes and Consequences of School Exclusions: Teachers, Parents and Schools' Perspectives*. London: Routledge.

Department for Education (DfE) (2019), 'Permanent and fixed-period exclusions in England: 2017–2018'. https://assets.publishing.service.gov.uk/media/5d3967a0ed915d0d0e7a82df/Permanent_and_fixed_period_exclusions_2017_to_2018_-_main_text.pdf

Department for Education (DfE) (2023), 'How we are helping to inspire primary school children about their future careers'. https://educationhub.blog.gov.uk/2023/01/05/how-we-are-helping-to-inspire-primary-school-children-about-their-future-careers

Dolean, D., Melby-Lervåg, M., Tincas, I., Damsa, C. and Lervåg, A. (2019), 'Achievement gap: Socioeconomic status affects reading development beyond language and cognition in children facing poverty'. *Learning and Instruction*, 63, 101218.

Early Intervention Foundation (2023), 'Why is it good for children and families?'. www.eif.org.uk/why-it-matters/why-is-it-good-for-children-and-families#:~:text=Early%20intervention%20can%20help%20children,and%20support%20good%20mental%20health

Education and Employers (2010), 'The point of partnership: The case for employer engagement in education'. www.educationandemployers.org/research/the-point-of-partnership-the-case-for-employer-engagement-in-education/

Education Endowment Foundation (EEF) (2019), 'Putting evidence to work: A school's guide to implementation'. https://files.eric.ed.gov/fulltext/ED612284.pdf

Education Endowment Foundation (EEF) (2021), 'Effective professional development: Guidance report'. https://educationendowmentfoundation.org.uk/education-evidence/guidance-reports/effective-professional-development

Education Endowment Foundation (EEF) (2023), 'The EEF guide to the pupil premium: How to plan, implement, monitor and sustain an effective strategy'. https://educationendowmentfoundation.org.uk/education-evidence/using-pupil-premium

Education Endowment Foundation (EEF) (2024), 'A school's guide to implementation: Guidance report'. https://educationendowmentfoundation.org.uk/education-evidence/guidance-reports/implementation

Erickson, H. L. (2002), *Concept-Based Curriculum and Instruction: Teaching Beyond the Facts*. London: Corwin Press.

Erickson, H. L., Lanning, L. A. and French, R. L. (2017), *Concept-Based Curriculum and Instruction for the Thinking Classroom*. London: Corwin Press.

Fiennes, C. (2012), *It Ain't What You Give, It's the Way That You Give It: Making Charitable Donations That Get Results*. Giving Evidence.

Fletcher-Wood, H. and Zuccollo, J. (2020), 'The effects of high-quality professional development on teachers and pupils: A rapid review and meta-analysis'. Education Policy Institute; Ambition Institute; Wellcome. https://epi.org.uk/wp-content/uploads/2020/02/EPI-Wellcome_CPD-Review__2020.pdf

Flouri, E. and Panourgia, C. (2012), 'Do primary school children's career aspirations matter? The relationship between family, poverty, career aspirations, and emotional and behavioural problems'. Institute of Education. https://cls.ucl.ac.uk/wp-content/uploads/2017/04/CLS-WP-20125-.pdf

Flutter, J. (2007), 'The contribution of pupil voice to school improvement: In England the relationship between policy and practice', *Research Papers in Education*, 22, (2), 133–149.

Forde, C., Torrance, D. and Angelle, P. S. (2021), 'Caring practices and social justice leadership: Case studies of school principals in Scotland and USA', *School Leadership & Management*, 41, (3), 211–228. DOI: 10.1080/13632434.2020.186652.

Francis-Devine, B. (2023), 'Poverty in the UK: Statistics'. House of Commons Library. https://researchbriefings.files.parliament.uk/documents/SN07096/SN07096.pdf

Gay, B., Sonnenschein, S., Sun, S. and Baker, L. (2021), 'Poverty, parent involvement, and children's reading skills: Testing the compensatory effect of the amount of classroom reading instruction. *Early Education and Development*, 32, (7), 981–993.

Gazeley, L. (2012), 'The impact of social class on parent-professional interaction in school exclusion processes: Deficit or disadvantage?' *International Journal of Inclusive Education*, 16, (3), 297–311.

Gill, K., Quilter-Pinner, H. and Swift, D. (2017), 'Making The Difference: Breaking the link between school exclusion and social exclusion'. Institute for Public Policy Research. www.ippr.org/articles/making-the-difference

Gladwell, C. (2021), 'The impact of educational achievement on the integration and wellbeing of Afghan refugee youth in the UK'. *Journal of Ethnic and Migration Studies*, 47, (21): 4914–4936.

Gladwell, C. and Chetwynd, G. (2018), 'Education for refugee and asylum seeking children: Access and equality in England, Scotland and Wales'. UNICEF. www.unicef.org.uk/wp-content/uploads/2018/09/Access-to-Education-report-PDF.pdf

Gorard, S., Siddiqui, N. and See, B. H. (2019), 'The difficulties of judging what difference the Pupil Premium has made to school intakes and outcomes in England'. *Research Papers in Education*, 36, (3), 1–25.

Gorard, S., Siddiqui, N. and See, B. H. (2021), 'Assessing the impact of Pupil Premium funding on primary school segregation and attainment'. *Research Papers in Education*, 37, (6), 992–1019.

Greany, T. and Brown, C. (2015), 'Partnerships between teaching schools and universities: Research report'. London Centre for Leadership in Learning. https://citeseerx.ist.psu.edu/document?repid=rep1&type=pdf&doi=2b246b15978e74618d435ef7d492ed2a1ef8afe7

Guskey, T. R. (2002), 'Professional development and teacher change'. *Teachers and Teaching: Theory and Practice*, 8, 381–391.

Hackman, D. A. and Farah, M. J. (2009), 'Socioeconomic status and the developing brain'. *Trends in Cognitive Science*, 13, (2), 65–73.

Hanson, J. L., Hair, N., Shen, D. G., Shi, F., Gilmore, J. H., Wolfe, B. L. and Pollak, S. (2013), 'Family poverty affects the rate of human infant brain growth'. *PLOS ONE*, 8, (12), e0146434.

Hanson, J. L., Nacewicz, B. M., Sutterer, M. J., Cayo, A. A., Schaefer, S. M., Rudolph, K. D., Shirtcliff, E. A., Pollak, S. D. and Davidson, R. J. (2015), 'Behavioral problems after early life stress: Contributions of the hippocampus and amygdala'. *Biological Psychiatry*, 77, (4), 314–323.

Harlen, W. (ed.) (2010), 'Principles and big ideas for science education'. Association for Science Education. www.ase.org.uk/bigideas

Harris, S. (2021), 'Crafting your curriculum with poverty in mind'. *SecEd*. www.sec-ed.co.uk/content/best-practice/crafting-your-curriculum-with-poverty-in-mind/#:~:text=Find%20your%20other%20curriculum%20architects,your%20curriculum%20intent%20and%20impact.

Harris, S. (2022), 'Poverty on the brain: Five strategies to counter the impact of disadvantage'. *SecEd*. www.sec-ed.co.uk/content/best-practice/poverty-on-the-brain-five-strategies-to-counter-the-impact-of-disadvantage-in-the-classroom

Harris, S. and Gordon, M. (2022) 'Breaking the cycle of poverty and exclusion'. *SecEd*. www.sec-ed.co.uk/content/best-practice/breaking-the-cycle-of-poverty-and- exclusion.

Hirsch, Jr., E. D. (1999), *The Schools We Need: And Why We Don't Have Them*. New York: Doubleday Publishing Group.

Horgan, G. (2007), 'The impact of poverty on young children's experience of school'. Joseph Rowntree Foundation. https://basw.co.uk/sites/default/files/resources/basw_93245-5_0.pdf

ImpactEd (2022), 'The Kemnal Academies Trust: ACE Evaluation Summary 2021-22'. www.impacted.org.uk/ace-evaluation-summary-2021-22

Jensen, E. (2009), *Teaching with Poverty in Mind: What Being Poor Does to Kids' Brains and What School Can Do About It*. Washington: ASCD.

Joseph Rowntree Foundation (2022), 'UK Poverty 2022: The essential guide to understanding poverty in the UK', www.jrf.org.uk/uk-poverty-2022-the-essential-guide-to-understanding-poverty-in-the-uk

Joseph Rowntree Foundation (2023), 'What is poverty?'. www.jrf.org.uk/about-us/what-is-poverty

Karpicke, J. D. (2009), 'Metacognitive control and strategy selection: Deciding to practice retrieval during learning'. *Journal of Experimental Psychology: General*, 138, (4), 469–486.

Kashefpakdel, E. and Percy, C. (2016), 'Career education that works: An economic analysis using the British Cohort Study'. *Journal of Education and Work*, 30, (3), 217–234.

Kashefpakdel, E., Rehill, J. and Hughes, D. (2018), 'What works? Career-related learning in primary schools'. Careers and Enterprise Company. www.careersandenterprise.co.uk/media/m42pwir3/what-works-in-primary.pdf

Kashefpakdel, E., Rehill, J. and Hughes, D. (2019), 'Career-related learning in primary: The role of primary teachers and schools in preparing children for the future'. www.educationandemployers.org/wp-content/uploads/2019/01/EdEmp_CareerPrimary-report_Jan2019_v5_INDV.pdf.

Kellett, M. and Dar, A. (2007), 'Children researching links between poverty and literacy'. Joseph Rowntree Foundation. https://oro.open.ac.uk/15368/1/JRF_report_eudcation_and_poverty.pdf

Kennedy, J. (1995), 'Debiasing the curse of knowledge in audit judgment'. *The Accounting Review*, 70, (2), 249–273.

Kennedy, S. (2010), 'Child Poverty Act 2010: A short guide'. House of Commons Library. https://commonslibrary.parliament.uk/research-briefings/sn05585

Lambrechts, A. A. (2020), 'The super-disadvantaged in higher education: Barriers to access for refugee background pupils in England'. *Higher Education*, 80, 803–822.

Leat, D., Reid, A. and Lofthouse, R. (2015), 'Teachers' experiences of engagement with and in educational research: What can be learned from teachers' views?'. *Oxford Review of Education*, 41, (2), 270–286.

Luo, L. and Stoeger, H. (2023), 'Unlocking the transformative power of mentoring for youth development in communities, schools, and talent domains'. *Journal of Community Psychology*, 51, 3067–3082.

Maslow, A. H. (1943), 'A theory of human motivation'. *Psychological Review*, 50, (4), 370–396.

Mazzoli-Smith, L. and Todd, L. (2016), 'Poverty Proofing the School Day: Evaluation and development report'. Research Centre for Learning and Teaching, Newcastle University. https://children-ne.org.uk/wp-content/uploads/2022/06/86F983AD-4159-4FE1-9F37-3B567F2182C2.pdf

Mazzoli-Smith, L. and Todd, L. (2019), 'Conceptualising poverty as a barrier to learning through "Poverty proofing the school day": The genesis and impacts of stigmatisation'. *British Educational Research Journal*, 45, 356–371.

McIntyre, J. (2023), 'Promoting the inclusion of refugee children in schools: Recommendations for secondary education policy in England'. Refugee Education UK; University of Nottingham. https://hubhere.org/wp- content/uploads/2023/11/STRIVE-Policy-Brief_full-version.pdf

McLeod, S. A. (2018), 'Maslow's hierarchy of needs'. *Simply Psychology*. www.simplypsychology.org/maslow.html

McMahon, M. and Watson, M. (2022) 'Career development learning in childhood: A critical analysis'. *British Journal of Guidance & Counselling*, 50, (3), 345–350.

McPhail, G. and Rata, E. (2015), 'Comparing curriculum types: "Powerful knowledge" and "21st Century learning". *New Zealand Journal of Educational Studies*, 51, (1), 53–68.

Montacute, R. and Cullinane, D. (2021), 'Research brief: Learning in lockdown'. The Sutton Trust. www.suttontrust.com/wp-content/uploads/2021/01/Learning-in-Lockdown.pdf

Montacute, R. and Cullinane, C. (2023), '25 years of university access: How access to higher education has changed over time'. The Sutton Trust. www.suttontrust.com/wp-content/uploads/2023/10/25-Years-of-University-Access.pdf

Mullen, C. and Kealy, W. (2013), 'Poverty in school communities'. *Kappa Delta Pi Record*, 49, 70–77.

Newbury-Birch, D. and Allan, K. (2020), *Co-Creating and Co-Producing Research Evidence: A Guide for Practitioners and Academics in Health, Social Care and Education Settings*. London: Routledge.

Noble, K. G., Houston, S. M., Brito, N. H. et al. (2015), 'Family income, parental education and brain structure in children and adolescents'. *Nature Neuroscience*, 18, 773–778.

Organisation for Economic Co-operation and Development (OECD) (2021a), 'Embedding values and attitudes in curriculum: Shaping a better future'. www.oecd.org/en/publications/embedding-values-and-attitudes-in-curriculum_aee2adcd-en.html

Organisation for Economic Co-operation and Development (OECD) (2021b), 'The future at five: Gendered aspirations of five-year-olds'. https://issuu.com/oecd.publishing/docs/future-at-five-gendered-aspirations-five-year-olds

Paget, A., Parker, C., Heron, J., Logan, S., Henley, W., Emond, A. and Ford, T. (2018), 'Which children and young people are excluded from school? Findings from a large British birth cohort study, the Avon Longitudinal Study of Parents and Children (ALSPAC)'. *Child: Care, Health and Development*, 44, (2), 285–296.

Pensiero, N., Kelly, A. and Bokhove, C. (2021), 'Learning inequalities during the Covid-19 pandemic: A longitudinal analysis using the UK Understanding Society 2020 and 2021 data'. University of Southampton. https://eprints.soton.ac.uk/450310/1/Formatted_covid_report.pdf

Perham, N. and Currie, H. (2014), 'Does listening to preferred music improve reading comprehension performance?' *Applied Cognitive Psychology*, 28, 279–284.

Perkins, S. C., Ho, S. S., Evans, G. W., Liberzon, I., Gopang, M. and Swain, J. E. (2024), 'Language processing following childhood poverty: Evidence for disrupted neural networks'. *Brain and Language*, 252, 105414.

Picton, I. and Clark, C. (2023), 'Children and young people's book ownership in 2023: A 10-year retrospective'. National Literacy Trust. https://nlt.cdn.ngo/media/documents/Book_ownership_in_2023_k6ovlWY.pdf

Prentice, C. M. (2022), 'Educators' interactions with refugee pupils: Knowledge, attitudes, and practices'. Thesis, University of Oxford. https://ora.ox.ac.uk/objects/uuid:6e82d545-a1d5-406d-801c-3afa47131664/files/d0z708w97v

Quigley, A. and Coleman, R. (2021), 'Improving literacy in secondary schools: Guidance report'. Education Endowment Foundation. https://educationendowmentfoundation.org.uk/education-evidence/guidance-reports/literacy-ks3-ks4

Rata, E. (2015), 'A pedagogy of conceptual progression and the case for academic knowledge'. *British Educational Research Journal*, 42, (1), 168–184.

Refugee Education UK (2023), 'Inclusive and Sustainable Promising Practices in Refugee Education (InSPPiRE): Learnings from case studies in high-income settings: Executive summary'. www.reuk.org/_files/ugd/d5aa55_497666c9c14 6409f8000d0a71537751e.pdf

Rich, P. R., Van Loon, M. H., Dunlosky, J. and Zaragoza, M. S. (2017), 'Belief in corrective feedback for common misconceptions: Implications for knowledge revision'. *Journal of Experimental Psychology: Learning, Memory, and Cognition*, 43, (3), 492–501.

Ridge, T. (2002), *Childhood Poverty and Social Exclusion: From a Child's Perspective*. Bristol: Policy Press.

Ridge, T. (2011), 'The everyday cost of poverty in childhood: A review of qualitative research exploring the lives and experiences of low-income children in the UK'. *Children and Society*, 25, (1), 73–84.

Roediger, H. L. and Karpicke, J. D. (2006), 'Test-enhanced learning: Taking memory tests improves long-term retention'. *Psychological Science*, 17, (3), 249–255.

Rowland, M. (2021), *Addressing Educational Disadvantage in Schools and Colleges: The Essex Way*. Essex: Unit Research School and Essex County Council.

Schmidt, K. L., Merrill, S. M., Gill, R., Miller, G. E., Gadermann, A. M. and Kobor, M. S. (2021), 'Society to cell: How child poverty gets "Under the Skin" to influence child development and lifelong health'. *Developmental Review*, 61, 100983.

School Partnerships Alliance (2022), 'School partnerships for impact guide: Laying the groundwork for enabling and promoting meaningful partnerships between different schools across the state and independent sectors'. https://schoolpartnershipsalliance.org.uk/s-p-a-guid

Sime, D. and Sheridan, M. (2014), 'You want the best for your kids: Improving educational outcomes for children living in poverty through parental engagement'. *Educational Research*, 56, (3), 327–342.

Simons, D. J. and Chabris, C. F. (1999), 'Gorillas in our midst: Sustained inattentional blindness for dynamic events'. *Perception*, 28, (9), 1059–74.

Simpson, E. (2023), 'Canary in the mine: What white working-class underachievement reveals about processes of marginalisation in English secondary education'. *International Studies in Sociology of Education*, 33, (2), 246–265.

Smith, B. (2015), *Mentoring At-Risk Pupils Through the Hidden Curriculum of Higher Education*. Plymouth: Lexington Books.

Sobel, D. (2018), *Narrowing the Attainment Gap: A Handbook for Schools*. London: Bloomsbury.

Taplin, D., Clark, H., Collins, E. and Colby, C. (2013), 'Theory of change technical papers: A series of papers to support development of theories of change based on practice in the field'. ActKnowledge. www.actknowledge.org/resources/documents/ToC-Tech-Papers.pdf

Teach First (2022), 'Stark destination gap: Disadvantaged pupils twice as likely to be out of work or education as their wealthier peers'. www.teachfirst.org.uk/press-release/destination-gap

Teach First (2024), 'UK STEM skills shortage "at risk of growing" as low-income parents fear for children's prospects'. www.teachfirst.org.uk/press-release/uk-stem-skills-shortage

Timperley, H., Wilson, A., Barrar, H, and Fung, I. (2007), *Teacher Professional Learning and Development: Best Evidence Synthesis Iteration (BES)*. Wellington, New Zealand: Ministry of Education.

Toth, K., Cross, L., Golden, S. and Ford, T. (2023), 'From a child who IS a problem to a child who HAS a problem: Fixed period school exclusions and mental health outcomes from routine outcome monitoring among children and young people attending school counselling'. *Child Adolescent Mental Health*, 28, 277–286.

Turner, S. (2016), *Bloomsbury CPD Library: Secondary Curriculum and Assessment Design*. London: Bloomsbury.

Wagle, U. R. (2008), 'Rethinking poverty: Definition and measurement'. *International Social Science Journal*, 54, (171), 155–165.

Wagmiller, R. L. (2015), 'The temporal dynamics of childhood economic deprivation and children's achievement'. *Child Development Perspectives*, 9, (3), 158–163.

Walton, G. M. and Cohen, G. L. (2011), 'A brief social-belonging intervention improves academic and health outcomes of minority students'. *Science*, 331, (6023), 1447–1451.

Wang, Q. and Zhang, H. (2014), 'Promoting teacher autonomy through university–school collaborative research'. *Language Teaching Research*, 18, (2), 222–241.

Wheelahan, L. (2010), *Why Knowledge Matters in the Curriculum: A Social Realist Argument*. Abingdon: Routledge.

Wikeley, F., Bullock, K., Muschamp, Y. and Ridge, T. (2007), 'Educational relationships outside school: Why access is important'. Joseph Rowntree Foundation. www.docs.hss.ed.ac.uk/education/outdoored/educational_relationships.pdf

Wiliam, D. (2013), 'Principled curriculum design'. SSAT. https://webcontent.ssatuk.co.uk/wp-content/uploads/2023/12/05151905/SSAT-Redesigning-Schooling-03-Principled-curriculum-design.pdf

Willingham, D. T. (2009), *Why Don't Pupils Like School? A Cognitive Scientist Answers Questions about How the Mind Works and What it Means for the Classroom*. San Francisco: Jossey-Bass.

Wood, E., Zivcakova, L., Gentile, P., Archer, K., De Pasquale, D. and Nosko, A. (2012), 'Examining the impact of off-task multi-tasking with technology on real-time classroom learning'. *Computers & Education*, 58, 365–374.

Young, M. and Muller, J. (2016), *Curriculum and the Specialisation of Knowledge: Studies in the Sociology of Education*. London: Routledge.